ENNETH GROBECKER, AIA   EVA GRYCZON
AVID W. HALL   MEGAN HAMLIN   PHILLIP
AN   JAMES HANSEN, AIA   ANTOINE HARB
RACEY HARDWICK   TIFFANY HARTLEY   LORI
NN HASHIMOTO   ANDRE HELFENSTEIN   JANE
ENDRICKS   GLEN ANTHONY HENSLEY
ESSICA S. HENSLEY   HANS HERST   CINDY
OEBINK   SHANNON HOLDERMAN   WILLIAM
UANG   JOOST HULSHOF   RONALD J.
UTCHENS, AIA   MATTHEW IMADOMI
ARYATI IMANTO   STEPHEN IP   CHACKO C.
ACOB   CHARLES JOHNSON   MOHAN JOSHI
EVIN JOYCE, AIA   ARLENE S. JUAN   PETER
NG C. KARUNG   LOUIS A. KAUFMAN, AIA
REG KEATING   ROBIN KERPER   FREDERICK
. KERZ, AIA   KAZUHIRO KIBUISHI   DO
YOUNG KIM   JOSHUA L. KIMMEL   JEANNE
INNEY   SATSUKI KITAGAWA   ANN M.
NUDSEN, AIA   MARY KOPITZKE   GARY G.
RENZ, AIA   PAMELA KU   RICHARD L. KUEI
ENDRA KUSUMA   DANIEL KWOK   JULIE
AMPRECHT   KIM LANDAU   ROI LAPEYRE
LISON LARSEN   MASI LATIANARA   MITCHELL
AWRENCE, AIA   CHARLES LEE   MANKI LEE
TELLA LEE   STEPHANIE LEEDOM   RAYMOND
EUNG   JILL LEWIS   PAUL LI   CHIN K. LIM, AIA
RIC H. LIN   I-JOEN LIN   FANG LIU   LEO
VSHETZ   KENNETH R. LONG, AIA   NANCY
ONG   DENISE LOZA   CHEN LU   FRANK LU   RNY
ADALE   CHRISTINE MAGAR   DARYL M.
AGUIRE, ANZIA   KLAYDEN MALEKPOURANI
UDY MARIN   STEVEN MCENTEE   CARMEL
CFAYDEN   KENNETH MCKENTLY   SABRINA
EDRANO   GAYLORD MELTON   ANGELA
ERCER   CARINNE MEYER   COLETTE MEYER
OUGLAS B. MEYER, AIA   FREDERICK MEYER
EELAM MIAN   ELLEN MILLER   BLYTHE
ILLION   HIROKO MIYAKE   ARNIE MOK
ATHERINE D. MORADO   YUNJOO NAMKOONG
ATTHEW NELSON   ALLETA NESBIT   LOURDES
ISHI   MICHELLE NISKALA   CINDY NG   UNG
GU   CHARLES W. "DUKE" OAKLEY, FAIA

JOHN ODA   STEVEN S. OH   MICHAEL J.
O'SULL   C.
OWEN   NDY
PANAM   RK
YOUNG   ADAM   PARK   ANGELITO
PASAMONTE   PURNIMA PATIL   CYNTHIA
PHAKOS   JOHN PHUNG   JOSE PIMENTAL
MARCO POLANCO   TREVOR POLLARD   ARRAN
PORTER   DAMON PORTER   BEVERLY POWELL
MOHAN PRADHAN   EVELYN PRINZ   MARIA
QUANDT   A. RACHO   JEROME RADIN   MARK
RANDOLPH   DAVID REDDY, AIA   TOM
ROBERTSON   EDWARD ROBISON   PATINA A.
RODGERS   YOUNGJOO ROH   MARIA ROMERO
TYMON ROS   BRIAN RUSSELL   KATE RUSSELL
FRANCINE SACCO   KAREN SAFER   TIM
SAKAMOTO   YASUYUKI SAKURAI   JAMES
SALAZAR   SONAL K. SANCHETI   JOSE SANCHEZ
SHAHAN SANOSSIAN   RICARDO SANTIA
KRISTI SCHNEIDER   JEFFREY SCHNEIDER
MARGARET SCHWARTZ   ANDREW SCOTT
LINDA SCOTT   LEONARDA SEWARD   MARK J.
SHAW   JOANN SHEU   EDWIN SIERRA   ARTIN T.
SIMONIAN   MARTA RECIO SLAGTER   AMY
SMITH   CHRIS SPIERINGS   ANDIE SQUIRES
OLESIA STEFURAK   ANDREA STEIN   YINGZI SU
FAY SVELTZ   CHIULING TA   ANNIE H. TAN
KANIT TANTIWONG   DELIA TORRES   RUBEN
TORRES   DIEMMI TRAN   PAUL TRAN   ANNE
TRELEASE   CHARLES C. TSAI   JULIA
TSCHIERSCH   LISA TUCKER   SHIGERU USAMI
MANUEL J. VARGAS   JON W. VASZAUSKAS
FRANK C. VENTURA JR.   SUZY VERNOFF   HUEY
VUONG   SYLVIA WALLIS   KEVIN WARD   EVA
WATERS   EVETTE WESTBROOK   GLENN
WILLIAMS   ANNA WIN, AIA   JOANNA W.
WONG   MARILYN WONG   ANNETTE WU
DANIELLE S.N. YAFUSO   LIBING YAN   LIMING
YANG   NUSHIN YAZDI   BILL YEE   CHIEN YEH
JULIAN YIP   LESLIE J. YOUNG   MEGAN
YOUNGER   IVY W. YUNG   MICHAEL ZAKIAN
HRAZTAN ZEITLIAN   MIN ZHUO

THE MASTER ARCHITECT SERIES

ALTOON + PORTER ARCHITECTS

SELECTED + CURRENT WORKS

images
Publishing

Published in Australia in 2006 by
The Images Publishing Group Pty Ltd
ABN 89 059 734 431
6 Bastow Place, Mulgrave, Victoria 3170, Australia
Tel: +61 3 9561 5544 Fax: +61 3 9561 4860
books@images.com.au
www.imagespublishing.com

Copyright © The Images Publishing Group Pty Ltd 2006
The Images Publishing Group Reference Number: 333

All rights reserved. Apart from any fair dealing for the purposes of private study, research, criticism or review as permitted under the Copyright Act, no part of this publication may be reproduced, stored in a retrieval system or transmitted in any form by any means, electronic, mechanical, photocopying, recording or otherwise, without the written permission of the publisher.

National Library of Australia Cataloguing-in-Publication entry:

Altoon + Porter Architects: selected and current works.

ISBN 1 876907 44 4.

1. Altoon + Porter Architects. 2. Architectural firms – California – Los Angeles.
3. Architecture, Modern.
(Series: Master architect series.)

720.979494

Coordinating editor: Robyn Beaver

Designed by The Graphic Image Studio Pty Ltd, Mulgrave, Australia
www.tgis.com.au

Digital production by Splitting Image Colour Studio Pty Ltd, Australia
Printed by Everbest Printing Co. Ltd. in Hong Kong/China

IMAGES has included on its website a page for special notices in relation to this and our other publications. Please visit www.imagespublishing.com

Every effort has been made to trace the original source of copyright material contained in this book. The publishers would be pleased to hear from copyright holders to rectify any errors or omissions.

The information and illustrations in this publication have been prepared and supplied by Altoon + Porter Architects. While all reasonable efforts have been made to ensure accuracy, the publishers do not, under any circumstances, accept responsibility for errors, omissions and representations express or implied.

Contents

4	**Altoon + Porter: Context is a value, not a style** by Morris Newman
7	**Essence, Context and Diversity** an essay by Ronald A. Altoon, FAIA

8 MOVEMENT
- 10 Sengkang Station
- 16 Buangkok Station
- 22 UCLA Parking Structure #3
- 26 The Shops at Tanforan

30 MATERIALITY
- 32 5700 Wilshire Boulevard Offices
- 36 444 South Flower Street Offices
- 44 MCA Universal Offices
- 48 Macy*s Prototype
- 52 2000 Residence
- 62 Echo Horizon School

67 **Bringing Discipline to Design** an essay by James F. Porter, AIA

68 CLIMATE AND TERRAIN
- 70 Ka'ahumanu Center
- 76 Bighorn Institute
- 78 The Gardens on El Paseo
- 83 Warringah Mall
- 86 Carrara Place Compound
- 98 Paramaz Avedisian Building
- 102 Exotic Animal Training and Management Facility, Moorpark College

107 **Collaboration and Construction** an essay by Gary K. Dempster, AIA

108 TECHNOLOGY
- 110 Fashion Show
- 116 UCSB California NanoSystems Institute
- 120 Central World Plaza
- 124 Auchan Competition
- 128 SetúCentre
- 132 Chodov Centrum

136 COMMUNITY
- 138 Knox City Centre
- 142 PacifiCenter
- 148 Yassenevo
- 150 Buchanan Galleries
- 152 Capitol Center
- 156 Adriatico Towers
- 158 Five Pillars
- 160 Victoria Gardens

167 **City Rooms as Civic Space** an essay by William J. Sebring, AIA

168 CIVICISM
- 170 Grand Avenue Urban Design Plan
- 176 Kowloon Station Development
- 178 Crocker Art Museum
- 182 Newport Harbor Art Museum

184 CULTURE
- 186 Taman Anggrek Condominiums
- 188 Botany Town Centre
- 194 Nieuw Hoog Catharijne
- 202 Les Portes de Gascogne
- 204 Al Mamlaka at Kingdom Centre

209 **Defining Legacy** an essay by James C. Auld, AIA

210 LEGACY
- 212 Dragon Tower
- 214 Felipe de Neve Branch Library
- 218 Siqueiros Mural Shade Structure
- 222 Arthur Ashe Student Health and Wellness Center, UCLA
- 226 John Wooden Recreation Center North and West Expansions, UCLA
- 230 USC School of Social Work Center
- 234 Southwestern University School of Law Library

- 240 Fractals of Architecture
- 248 Chronology of Projects
- 252 Design Awards
- 254 Consultants and Collaborators

Altoon + Porter: Context is a value, not a style

By Morris Newman

We are sitting in Ronald Altoon's living room. It is a tall, white volume detailed in natural wood, with the Southern California sunlight streaming in from four sides. The architect has arrived home only two hours ago on a red-eye flight from Alaska. In 24 hours, he is scheduled to fly again, this time to Europe.

Neither tired nor disoriented, he eagerly sits down over coffee to go through his list of current and recent projects. For the next four hours, he talks about everything—everything, that is, except the details of their theoretical positions. With projects of many kinds—transit stations in Singapore and the Netherlands, high-rise housing in Manila and Jakarta, retail in Riyadh and Moscow—he may simply be too busy.

Then again, he may not take stylistic labels per se very seriously.

"Some people call themselves Modernists, while others say they are Postmodernists," says Altoon.

As for his own firm, Altoon + Porter, "we are contextualists," he says.

In a single word, the architect has outlined the working philosophy of the firm. Contextualism, however, in the way Altoon uses the word, becomes something fairly complex. He does not use the word in the commonly understood sense, that of designing to conform with existing buildings on the site. His notion of contextualism is far more inclusive.

For Altoon + Porter, context is a value. This approach puts human comfort and well-being at the top of the scale, and addresses plan making as well as building technology to that end.

Context, of course, is not a single factor, which is why stylistic contextualism, by itself, is superficial. Context is many factors—culture, climate, building technology, urbanism—working together as a system.

Climate could be called the first context. As readers of *The Prodigious Builders* by Bernard Rudofsky will know, much of the genius of vernacular architecture lies in its direct response to climate. Showing a commitment to natural light, natural ventilation and sustainable construction long before such issues became fashionable among large firms, Altoon + Porter constantly looks for opportunities to bring the primary elements of human comfort into its design work.

In the Paramaz Avedisian Building at the American University of Armenia in Yerevan, the firm has adapted the outwardly looking International-style elevation into a thermal chimney for passive heating and cooling. This strategy makes particular sense in Armenia, where the electrical grid can be unreliable. In a different way, in a different climate, tall retail passages in Les Portes de Gascogne in Toulouse, France, not only echo the classic typology of the Milan Galleria, but also allow plentiful air circulation, as well as natural light from a continuous row of clerestory windows.

In the sensuous climate of Maui, where the thermometer reading is often close to skin temperature, Altoon + Porter designed what is essentially an open-air retail center, in which prevailing breezes provide natural cooling, while a high-tech tensile roof protects shoppers from the direct sun. One of Altoon's favorite compliments regarding the Ka'ahumanu Center was the unsolicited comment of a native Hawaiian woman who approached him one day, and said of the center, "this is our place." It was her place not merely to shop, but to feel a sense of ownership, as well. And while the arid climate of Palm Springs in Southern California is very unlike Hawaii, the same principles apply to The Gardens at El Paseo, where Altoon + Porter's architects have arranged the buildings in a way to induce breezes through the open-air passages of this outdoor shopping center in the high desert.

In a very different building in the same region, the Bighorn Institute—a complex devoted to the preservation of the endangered bighorn sheep—the thick walls and high ceilings of the stucco building provide natural ventilation, while high, narrow clerestory windows on the north and east provide natural light without adding heat.

Even in the constrained setting of a high-rise office building in Los Angeles in the 444 South Flower Street Offices, where the closest thing to nature is the daylight from perimeter windows, Altoon + Porter has capitalized on that sole amenity by turning the typical office layout on its head, providing work places for staff by the windows, while locating managers in glass-lined offices away from the corners which are reserved for conference use.

Culture is another important context, particularly at a time when the long debate about regionalism and cultural identity in architecture is strong, predominantly in the fast-developing nations in Asia and the Middle East, as well as in Europe, where an insensitive building can stir local resentment and result in commercial failure.

In Toulouse, an ancient farming region, local patterns of land use encourage builders to leave a patch of green building, rather than clustering structures together. Accordingly, in the plan of the above-mentioned Gascogne retail project, the wings of the shopping center reach out into green fields like a hand with open fingers. In Moorpark, a small city north of Los Angeles, the siting of the Exotic Animal Training & Management Program at Moorpark College echoes the hilltop siting of many houses in this bedroom community.

The quietest intervention that Altoon + Porter has designed is intended for Olvera Street, a busy shopping area amid the old adobes and masonry buildings that are among the oldest and most historic in Los Angeles. Several years ago, workmen discovered a faded mural by the Mexican artist David Alfaro Siqueiros (1896–1974), which had been boarded over by a patron angered by the overt political content of the work. To enable visitors to see the mural while protecting it from the destructive effects of sunlight, Altoon + Porter proposed the Sun Shade Structure for the Siqueiros Mural, a simple, open-air structure that allows visitors to look down on the mural from a second-story height, while providing a protective roof for both visitors and artwork.

Another act of quiet contextualism, in a sense, was the adaptive reuse of the former Bullock's Wilshire Department store—perhaps the single greatest glory of the Art Deco style in Los Angeles—into the Southwestern University School of Law Library. In this respectful and minimally disruptive reuse of a culturally significant building, Altoon + Porter has located most of the book stacks in areas where clothing and other merchandise had been displayed in Parkinson & Parkinson's 1931 masterpiece, leaving the splendid Jock Peters' murals and detailing untouched, except for protective restoration.

The loudest of the firm's buildings, on the other hand, is Fashion Show in Las Vegas. This high-end shopping center responds confidently to the hallucinatory excess of the Las Vegas Strip, where a building needs an extremely strong voice to be "heard" at all. Almost equal in intensity is the Central World Plaza, a retail centerpiece of what Altoon describes as the Times Square of Thailand. The coup de theatre here is a 350-meter-long media wall with LED screens, lasers and "talking" ticker-tape signs.

In cases where stylistic contextualism is called for, such as the area between the California State Capitol and the American River in Sacramento, Altoon + Porter has found the tasteful line between respect and stylistic independence. The Crocker Art Museum master plan takes on the symmetry and stone, if not the literal Classicism, of the nearby State Capitol and other government buildings. More literal, and perhaps a wittier comment on context, is the Arthur Ashe Center, in which the lower portions of the building are rendered in the red-brick Collegiate Gothic that mirrors much of the campus, while the two upper stories suddenly change into white stucco—a mordant commentary on stylistic dislocations, both on campus and in Los Angeles as a whole.

Cultural context is an overarching issue in Riyadh, where gender segregation is a matter of the strictest religious and civil law. At the same time, Riyadh is a wealthy community with a high level of interest in Western fashion, even if that fashion can be displayed only within the confines of one's own home. At Al Mamlaka at Kingdom Centre, the third floor of an otherwise Western-style shopping mall is devoted entirely, and exclusively, to women. In this protective environment, women may doff their chador for a few hours and shop with American abandon, while preserving Saudi modesty.

If context means respect for climate, site, and culture, then the word might also be expanded to mean a sensitivity to that which is needed on the site, but does not yet exist. Like many architects with global practices, Altoon + Porter often finds itself working in cities that are growing at a frenzied rate, and where urban design is either lax or simply non-existent. In such cities, urban sites are often fragmentary, disconnected from older parts of the city and unsatisfying.

Every building, in a small way, is an act of urban design, contributing to the well-being (or the dysfunction) of the city at large. Altoon + Porter is unusual among international firms, in going out of its way to identify urban problems and to address them, within the confines of a given design problem.

A prime example of addressing urban conditions is the Adriatico Tower in Manila. In one sense, the program of the building—a complex of four, high-security residential towers connected by a low-rise plinth of retail space—is symptomatic of the anxiety of middle-class home owners in a city of economic disparity. Sensing the need for truly public, pedestrian streets, Altoon + Porter makes a public gesture by providing an extra-wide sidewalk across the length of the project, spanning the length of a city block. Altoon says he hopes the sidewalk will provide a pattern for neighboring blocks to follow, leading eventually to a continuous, pedestrian-oriented street.

A similar problem in a very different city is the Nieuw Hoog Catharijne in Utrecht, The Netherlands, where the assignment was to create a residential-and-retail complex at Holland's busiest rail station. The ambitious design problem required the architects to span a proposed reconstructed former canal, providing a pedestrian bridge between the rail station and the city's Medieval Square. Here, the most inspired part of Altoon + Porter's solution, arguably, is the creation of a "city room" immediately above the canal within the enclosed bridge, which provides excellent views of the city and canal, while offering a much-needed moment of orientation to visitors before entering the convention complex.

The Buchanan Galleries in central Glasgow is a design problem that the late Colin Rowe would have relished: inserting a modern building into a historic district with Victorian and Georgian architecture, in a part of the city where three different urban grids come together. The collision of those grids threatens a sense of lack of clarity and resolution in an active redevelopment district. Treating the Glasgow design problem as one of urban connections, Altoon + Porter provided a master plan for a shopping center that at once mediates and connects two different urban grids, by connecting the existing Queen Street Train Station and the existing landmark Dundas Hose building, three university campuses and a cultural center. The project holds the promise not only of knitting together an urban district, but restoring activity that had been the traditional mainstay of this part of downtown Glasgow.

A different urban design problem can be found at Yassenevo, a suburb of Moscow, where acres of identical apartment blocks have been built in the dreariest Stalinist style. Here, the need is not to complement the context but to change it. Working at the mid-rise scale of the apartment complexes, Altoon + Porter has provided curtain wall buildings for office space and an entertainment center. A related project, philosophically, is the Chodov Centrum in Prague, where a 64,000-square-foot retail center works hard to disguise the monotony of a Soviet-era housing complex.

Altoon + Porter's design for Grand Avenue in Los Angeles takes on a difficult problem of reconnecting on a bridge-like street—the site of the city's new Rafael Moneo-designed cathedral and the Frank Gehry-designed concert hall—with the rest of downtown. Collaborating with those and other architects, Altoon + Porter offers a master plan to provide a broader plaza in front of the concert hall and existing Music Center to accommodate crowds, while connecting the street with a 17-acre park directly east of the Gehry building. By connecting Grand Avenue to the park, the Altoon + Porter scheme re-activates the long-neglected Los Angeles Mall, a green carpet stretching three blocks from the concert hall to the city's pyramid-topped City Hall on the west.

In some cities that are new and/or under-developed, developers may wish to create mixed-use districts that effectively serve as town centers. The challenge to architects is both stimulating and perilous: how to fashion a town center from scratch, without looking hopelessly hokey or ersatz?

The very idea of Victoria Gardens in Rancho Cucamonga, California, would probably make purists bar the door: in an affluent community in the desert east of Los Angeles, the developer Forest City hired Altoon + Porter to revise the master plan and design the majority of buildings for a mixed-use complex. The "back story" is that Victoria Gardens is the small-town Main Street that never existed, but could have grown up on this site, if the town had followed a slower pattern of urban growth.

The brilliant solution, covering twelve city blocks, provides new shopping streets in a variety of widths and scales, like a genuine urban district. Victoria Gardens is unique, at least in California, for actually connecting with the existing street grid, as opposed to "lifestyle centers," pseudo-streets that often bear little relation to the surrounding urban pattern. The façades, ranging from the ostensible ruins of a Craftsman home, a feed lot for cattle and buildings from different eras from the 1930s to the present, are done with stylistic accuracy and quiet wit. True, Victoria Gardens is a stage set, but this Pinnochio downtown has enough underlying under-design quality to mature into a "real boy." A similar exercise in the making of an instant downtown is the Botany Town Centre in Auckland, New Zealand.

As mentioned earlier, Altoon + Porter treats context as an approach to the entire set of design problems. Rather than concerning itself with self-referential issues of style, Altoon + Porter's practice seeks, within the constraints of program and budget, for ways to maximize the well-being of users. Another way of putting is that the firm searches for the best possible relationship among buildings, people, and urban surroundings, from the point of view of human experience. For readers, especially those previously unaware of the technical and geographic range of the firm, this book documents the results of a fruitful search.

ESSENCE, CONTEXT AND DIVERSITY

Mankind creates. Creativity brings joy. People express themselves differently from place to place, contingent on the forces that make them collectively individual. We celebrate such difference as we design to meet very real human needs.

With these beliefs as the foundation for our design philosophy, we study the dynamics at the root of those differences. Our work recognizes and accepts the constraints of context as the *a priori* determinant of architectural form. For us no single, signature architectural style would embrace the rich diversity of conditions. Places exist as nature has crafted them and mankind has enriched them. Here, we begin.

Context is defined as the *natural forces* of sun, wind, water, and climate; the *geographic forces* of geology and landscape; the *historic forces* of built form, material, tradition, and craft; the *social forces* of economics, politics, religion, and culture. We interpret these forces in response to each site, each condition, each community. Although we design in response to place, our ends are always greater as we seek to enhance that place.

Many aspects define and separate cultures—religious, social, economic, political. Collectively, they form the essence of mankind. My teacher, Louis Kahn, spoke of essence. In his work he expressed the concept primarily through the design of institutional buildings. In our work essence emerges in a less formal, but equally assertive, fashion. We explore the issues of essence in places of learning, of commerce, of transit. Often our work addresses the essence of city itself—of civic life and community.

Our constant, overarching concern is to design projects that are essentially of the place and the people who will use and enjoy them. Our projects are also unmistakably of our time. We build on our architectural heritage yet leave an ever-richer legacy as a result of our efforts.

Concerns for the natural environment and for natural order equally shape our designs. My studies with Ralph Knowles at the University of Southern California, and Ian McHarg at the University of Pennsylvania made sustainable design a central concern from the earliest days of our practice. Decades before sustainable standards were established, our work endeavored to respect limited natural resources and to be energy efficient. Today we are committed to revitalizing traditional town centers, to creating versatile, efficient mixed-use projects, and adapting existing building stock for new purposes—to creating a sustainable future.

The work of this practice is as diverse as the places we build, our global clients, and the users of our designs. As agile and hand-on practitioners, we have evolved a culture of design collaboration between the partners and colleagues, where the best idea prevails in the better interest of those we ultimately serve. It is a powerful culture rooted in sensitivity, respect, and appreciation and it enriches our work in projects large and small, for public entities and private clients around the world.

**Ronald A. Altoon, FAIA,
UIA, FRAIC, Hon. FRAIA,
Hon. JIA, Hon FCAM, Hon UAR**
Partner

MOVEMENT

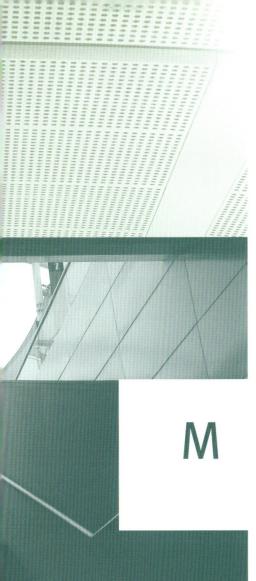

Multi-modal transportation systems with multi-tasking travelers have created new challenges for the design of public infrastructure and gathering spaces. Altoon + Porter Architects understands that new stations must meet the aspirational goals of their builders, whether public agencies or private developers. At the same time, they need to be models of efficient design that allow for easy navigation through spaces where passengers can make visual and physical connections for the next train or for next door.

Design 1997/Completion 2004

Land Transportation Authority

Two-level transit station

Glass, stainless steel

SENGKANG STATION
SINGAPORE

As one of the 12 stations that comprise Singapore's Northeast Line Expansion, Sengkang Station is one component of a new transportation system that embodies Singapore's commitment to world-class infrastructure. This multi-modal station has a distinctly urban character that is defined by its location at the juncture of a master planned district that includes mixed-use development, a bus depot, taxi station, the regional light-rail system above-ground, and the MRT subway below.

Simplicity of form and clarity of organization facilitate the movement of passengers between the various functions of the station and the adjacent office and residential development. Visual connections to the sun and sky are reinforced throughout all levels of the project. A sweeping, oval-shaped canopy shields the roof-level platforms of the light-rail system, while large expanses of glass allow light to flow down to the mezzanine and subway platforms. The canopy is raised on tall columns, creating an airy, open interior where escalators move passengers efficiently to their various destinations.

Entrances and pedestrian bridges, covered with a Teflon-coated fabric that was used for the first time in Singapore, establish a distinctive image for the transportation system. The fabric provides protection from both the sun and the brief tropical showers that occur throughout the region.

2

3

1 Mezzanine lobby level
2 3D perspective
3 Entry to subway platform

4

5

4 Exterior elevation
5 Public lobby
6 Entry to street level

6

Sengkang Station 13

7 Mezzanine level plan
8 Street level plan
9 LRT platform level plan
10 LRT platform level
11 Vertical transport system

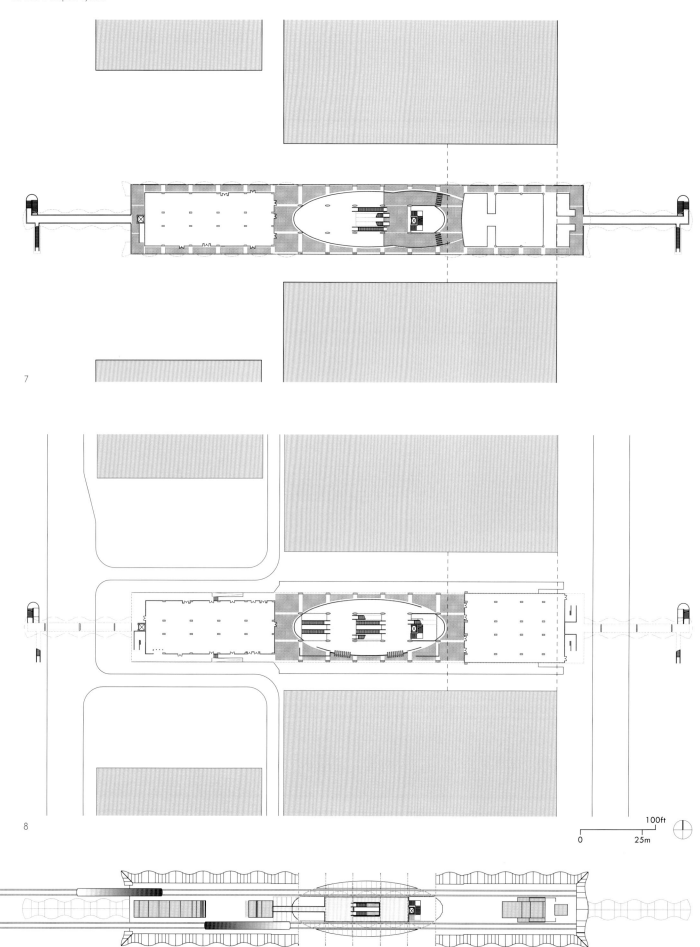

10

11

1 Canopy detail
2 Street level
3 Perspective
4 Drop-off platform

Design 1997/Completion 2005

Land Transportation Authority

Two-level transit station with tensile fabric-covered platform

Steel, Teflon-coated fiberglass, stainless steel panels, glass

BUANGKOK STATION
SINGAPORE

A suburban station that is part of Singapore's Northeast Line Expansion, Buangkok Station is sited in a high-density residential estate filled with multi-story towers. The placement of the station is indicative of the country's commitment to providing state-of-the-art public services to all its inhabitants.

In conformance with Singapore's active civil defense program, the station was built entirely below grade with public entrances straddling the high-speed roadway that runs above the station.

Taut wings of Teflon-coated fabric shield pedestrians from the elements and gather them into a central public hall that provides shelter for the access points and passageways. Inside, the station's open layout and decorated surfaces create a comfortable environment that softens the effects of the underground location, and the low ceilings required by military regulations. Warm artificial lighting penetrates the public spaces and the platforms that also double as an underground crosswalk for pedestrians.

Because the station is submerged within the landscape, the tented canopies give the project a public visibility and create an image that is visible from afar. The fabric structures create a beacon within the countryside, especially when the canopies are illuminated at night. By day the canopies soften the transition into the bright equatorial sun for emerging passengers.

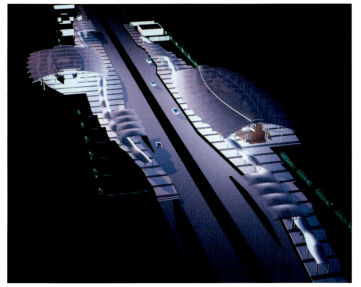

3

4

5

6

7

5 Outdoor drop-off
6 Concourse level
7 Platform level
8 Vertical transport

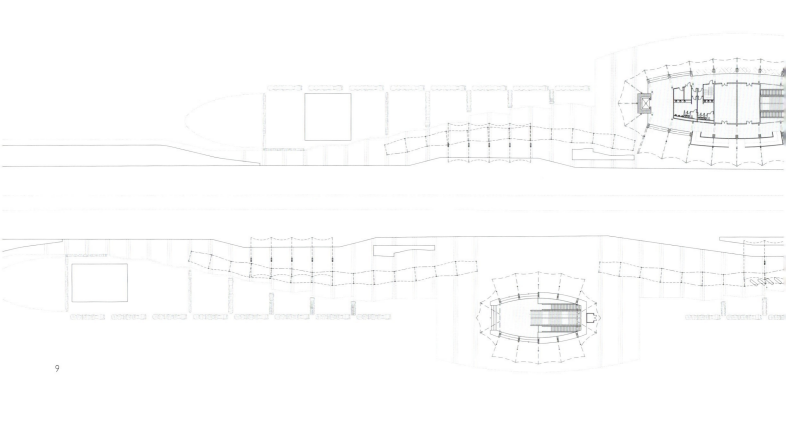

9

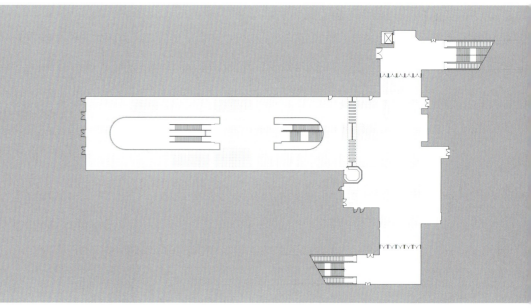

10

11

9 Street level plan
10 Concourse level plan
11 Canopy detail
12 Elevation
13 View to street

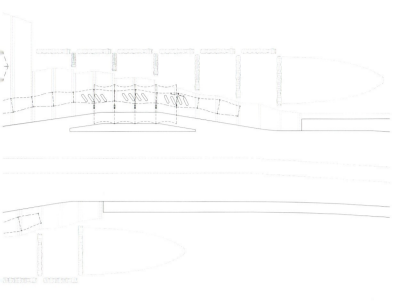

12

13

Buangkok Station

Design 1995/Completion 1995

University of California, Los Angeles Programs Design and Construction

7-story addition; 700 additional spaces

Steel structure, metal, masonry, concrete

UCLA Parking Structure #3
Los Angeles, California

1 Tower elevation
2 Site plan

This project expanded an existing parking structure by adding seven levels of parking and 845 parking spaces. The site is located at the edge of the UCLA campus, facing the elegant neighborhoods of Bel Air and Holmby Hills. Even though the parking structure was significantly expanded, careful planning and design both reduced the impact of the large facility along the residential streetscape, and created a new gateway to the UCLA campus.

To create a sense of arrival, the stair tower for vertical circulation was pulled out and away from the parking structure, creating a signature element for the building. Much like a campanile or freestanding bell tower commonly found on Italian buildings, it creates an appropriate marker that identifies the project as part of UCLA's Romanesque campus.

The use of specific materials and colors, arches, and patterning for the new parking structure and the tower also creates visual connections to the campus. Although larger than the previous structure, the new parking facility is a more sensitive, friendlier neighbor to the surrounding residential community.

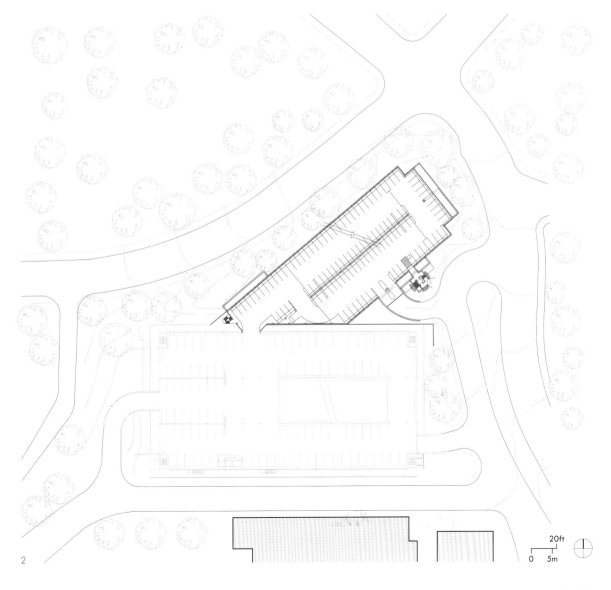

3 View from street
4 Tower detail
5 Masonry detail

UCLA Parking Structure #3   25

1 View from El Camino to main entrance plaza
2 West elevation
3 Main entrance
4 Ceiling detail
5 Elevation

1

2

Design 1999/Completion 2005

Wattson-Breevast

1,100,000 square feet

Steel structure, stone tile floor, drywall, metal ceiling, glass curtainwall

THE SHOPS AT TANFORAN
SAN BRUNO, CALIFORNIA

The 1.1-million-square-foot expansion of Tanforan Park Mall transforms the suburban shopping center into a multi-modal, mixed-use commercial complex, establishing a new model for community development in California. Located 30 miles south of San Francisco and one mile north of San Francisco International Airport, The Shops coincide with the expansion of the Bay Area Rapid Transit (BART) system and the construction of a new BART station adjacent to the site. New amenities include additional stores, restaurants, a multi-screen cinema, and structured parking.

The large-scale complex showcases grand civic spaces and transit-related retail opportunities that are closely linked to the BART station and the surrounding neighborhood. An outdoor plaza with restaurants, a bookstore, and a water feature provides access to the complex from the street. Inside the redesigned concourses, two levels of shops are organized around a spacious, light-filled central courtyard that connects to the BART station.

The Shops incorporate state-of-the-art energy efficient measures that conform to the LEED rating system of the US Green Building Council. Sustainable construction strategies include the use of recycled locally produced building products, as well as high-efficiency fixtures and mechanical systems that reduce the costs of lighting and cooling.

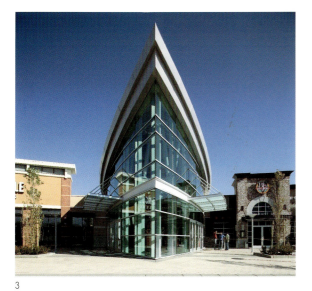

3

4

5

6   Northeast court
7   Southwest entrance
8   Food court
9   Ceiling detail

6

7

8
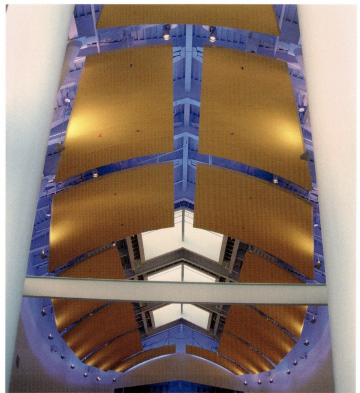
9

The Shops at Tanforan   29

MATERIALITY

While the work of Altoon + Porter Architects derives from a formal order that gives shape to program requirements, the firm finds inspiration in the material qualities of the building blocks. From the elemental play of solid and void, of transparency and opacity, of light and shadow, to the sophisticated employment of a new building product, the design exploits the potential of the material. Layered skins, revealed spaces, juxtaposed surfaces, and surprise detail are all part of the architects' material lexicon.

1

2

3

Design 1990/Completion 1991

Wilshire Courtyard

13,500 gross square feet

Drywall, glass

5700 Wilshire Boulevard Offices
Los Angeles, California

The goal was the redesign of ordinary speculative office space in the Wilshire corridor, LA's emerging entertainment district, into a highly creative work environment for a growing architectural firm. The program called for workspace for 80 people with private offices, meeting rooms, kitchens, gallery, storage, graphics center, library, and flexible work areas in 13,700 square feet of space.

Careful planning captured all of the usable space, although 33 percent was separated by an exit corridor and compromised by a change of level. Simple planes of drywall suspended from the structural framework created "clouds" that float like paper to transform the stiff aspect of the office building and to define work areas and private offices. All open and private work spaces are oriented to adjacent outside courtyards, while support spaces like storage, the graphics center, and meeting space are located near the interior core of the building.

The introduction of light was a critical component of the design and included large clerestories and punched openings that allow views and natural light to penetrate. The "clouds" also function as large reflectors to maximize the indirect lighting that fills the 14-foot-high space.

4

1 Custom lighting
2 Reception lobby
3 Reception
4 Circulation
5 Central office

5

6 Floor plan
7 Workspace
8 Conference room

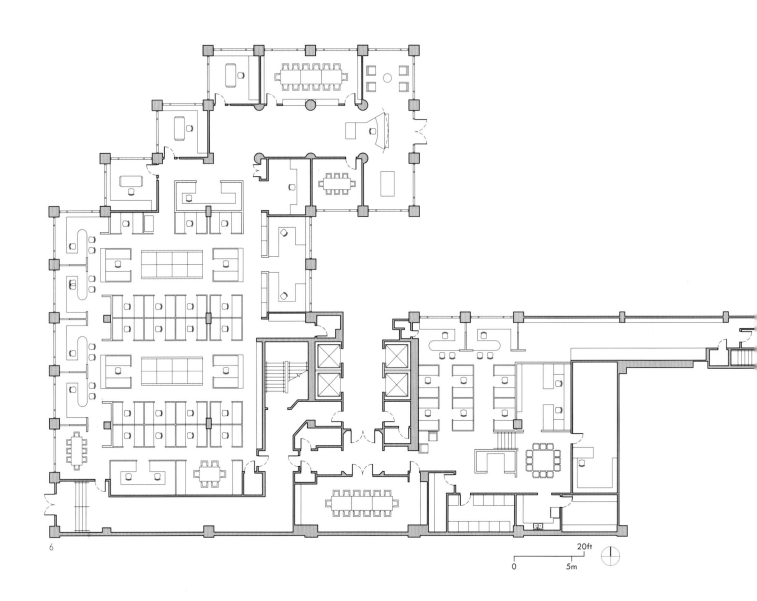

7

8

5700 Wilshire Boulevard Offices 35

1 Meeting area
2 Entrance to stairs
3&4 Meeting room
5 Reception

1

2

3

Design 1999/Completion 2000

Altoon + Porter Architects

28,000 square feet

Drywall, glass, perforated aluminum

444 South Flower Street Offices
Los Angeles, California

Two interconnecting penthouse floors in the heart of Los Angeles' financial district offered the structure and space the architectural firm needed to transform speculative offices into its own sophisticated workspace. Leveraging the views and light, the designers developed a plan that put the architects' workstations near the window walls, installed glazing on enclosed offices and situated conference rooms at the corners for firm-wide use.

The design also took advantage of the column-free space to lift the ceiling between the beams into coffers to create an open, light-filled space. A sleek palette of materials and soothing colors provides an inviting workspace and a suitable backdrop for display models and images of the firm's work. An inventive use of efficient and inexpensive twin tube fluorescent fixtures creates an elegant lighting system that reflects the light to enhance the volume of the space.

Materials include a black granite and stone floor, flame finished and polished; glass elevator lobby; a perforated stainless steel ceiling; drywall and reused wood walls from a previous tenant.

4

5

6

7

8

9

6 View to reception
7 Custom ceiling with light fixture
8 Conference room
9 View to private office
10 Reception desk
11 Workspace
12 Ceiling detail

10

11

12

13

14

15

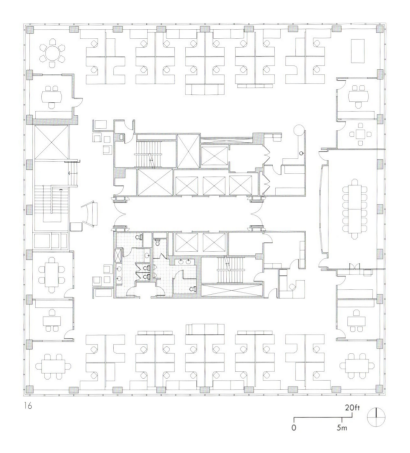

16

17

13 Ceiling detail
14 View to reception
15 Elevator lobby
16 Floor plan
17 Conference room

444 South Flower Street Offices

20

21

18&19 Reception gallery
20 Work wall
21 Elevator lobby to reception

1 Elevator lobby
2 Entry corridor
3 Reception desk

Design 1993/Completion 1995

MCA Universal

130,000 square feet

Gypsum board, glass

MCA Universal Offices
Universal City, California

The headquarters for the executives and creative staff of MCA Universal Studios' CityWalk entertainment complex consolidates the functions of many different administrative departments on the lot. The building contains space for many functions, including accounting, training, uniform claims, ride operations, merchandising, food services, television development, corporate sponsorship, and planning and development.

The company's corporate offices are located on a campus where each building has a distinct image that represents the character of each studio group. In keeping with the spirit, the interiors of this headquarters building have architectural voices that express the singular functions of each department, while common vocabularies and layouts create a coherent identity.

Bold color schemes, curved entryways, irregular spaces, and unusual details reflect the creative content of the occupants' work. Typical interior elements such as wall panels, light fixtures, and floor surfaces are rendered in a mix of materials, such as metal, treated glass, and wood veneer.

Individual departments branch off from the office lobbies that establish a central focus for each floor. The entrances to the departments act as "storefronts" where each office can display artwork, props, and other elements that relate to the unique nature of their work.

3

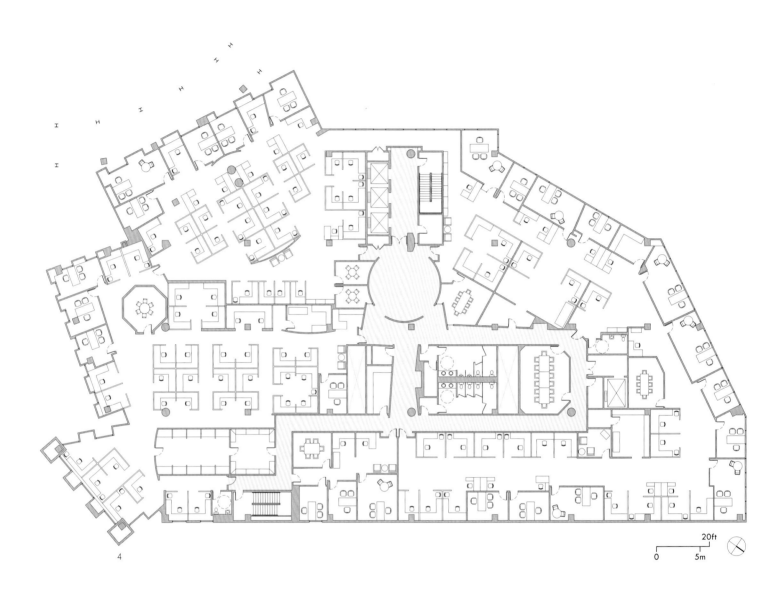

4   Floor plan
5   Circulation
6   Passageway
7   Lighting detail

5

6

7

MCA Universal Offices 47

Design 1998/Completion 2001

Federated Department Stores, Inc.

210,000 square feet

Steel structure, glass, eifs, aluminum, tiles, fine wood paneling

1   Main façade
2   Isometric perspective

Macy*s Prototype
Roseville and Lakewood, California

The Roseville and Lakewood department stores are upscale prototypes for Macy's that reposition the national retailer into the 21st century and create greater visibility in competitive suburban markets. The two designs use a vocabulary of shared elements—such as solid and transparent walls, portals, columns, and canopies—that can be easily reassembled to fit the contextual demands of the local sites.

The stores' forward-looking imagery redefines the Macy's brand as contemporary and chic. The exterior façades of the two buildings combine glass and masonry surfaces that are juxtaposed but remain physically distinct, creating a layered effect that diminishes their large volumes. Entrances are defined by glazed openings and delicate metal canopies that draw people inside, and corners of the buildings are demarcated by vertical elements rendered in stone. This complementary mix of textures and colors creates a recognizable identity for the retailer.

Details enhance the sequence of arrival and movement throughout the stores. Like the exterior of the buildings, the interior spaces feature smooth planes of solid and transparent materials, including glass, wood veneer, and metal finishes. Large open spaces are divided by retail counters, display areas, and columns to create a natural wayfinding system for customers.

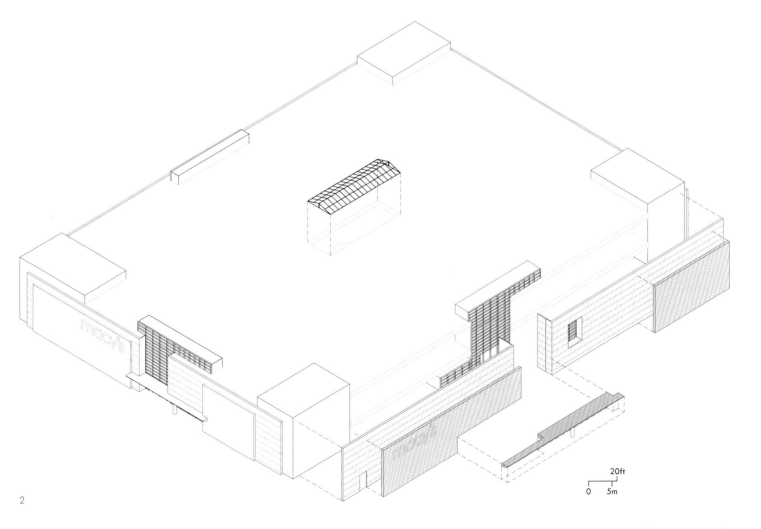

3 New façade
4 Illuminated view
5 Entry elevation

5

Macy*s Prototype 51

Design 1998/Completion 2000

Private owners

5135 square feet

2000 Residence
Los Angeles, California

Opposite, 2 Main living area

The 1950s standard issue California suburban ranch-style house was reinvented in a series of renovations and expansions that created a more formal plan for the space. Arranging the living spaces along a clearly defined axis brings a sense of organization and grace to the home. The addition of a high vaulted ceiling opens up the living and dining area and creates an opportunity to provide lighting from four directions.

Subtleties in the design are inspired by the work of the early California modernist architect Rudolph Schindler (planar solids and voids) and Craftsman architects Greene & Greene (rhythm, 18-inch grid). Architectural elements, placed indoors and out, act more as furnishings than as functional components: the free-standing constructionist fireplace centers the room and links to the outside and the entry; the 24-foot by 18-foot "shoji screen" display wall hosts collections of fine arts and crafts; and the suspended wooden "boat hull" light fixtures recall Scandinavian symbols used to keep souls alive while at a distance.

Simple materials provide subtle backdrops for the sculptural qualities of the rooms' custom-designed furnishings. The minimalist aesthetic is an elegant backdrop for larger art works that hang in spaces defined by volumes of light.

Beyond the glass walls and doors of the house a series of redwood decks and inclined trellises embrace the lush landscape to create an outdoor room beside the pool and extend the inside out and the outside in.

3   Pool and patio
4   Trellised garden
5   View to dining area

6

7

6 Display gallery
7 Fireplace with glass mantel
8 Ground floor plan
9 Living area

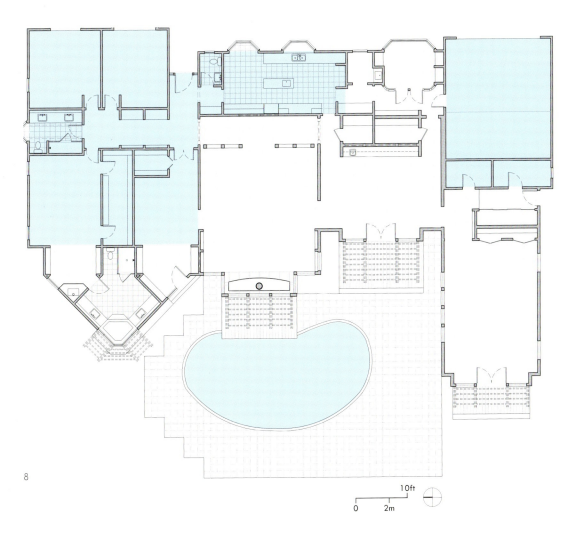

2000 Residence 57

10 Bath
11 Master bath
12 & 14 Formal dining area
13 Custom light fixture

10

11

13

14

15

16

17

15 Gallery
16 View to the garden
17 Kitchen

1 Library and classroom façade
2 Library and classroom exterior

Design 1992/Completion 1996

Echo Horizon Foundation

15,000 square feet

Exterior cement, plaster, steel trellis, glass

Echo Horizon School
Culver City, California

The 1926 campus of the Echo Horizon School, a private K–6 school in Culver City, California, required an expansion and a seismic upgrade. The school was first rebuilt after being damaged in the Long Beach earthquake of 1933. In 1987, the school sustained structural damage from the Whittier earthquake. The original building, designated by the city as a "significant" local structure, was appreciated by many. However, near neighbors, with views of the rear of the school, found little to praise in the architecture.

Expansion plans for the school, which educates hearing-impaired children without isolating them from hearing students, called for eight new classrooms as well as a library and outdoor play yards on a constrained site. At the same time, the school wanted to present to the community an appealing new face that harmonized with the original architecture.

The design solution is a wraparound addition that envelops the north, east, and south sides of the building with a new, formal structure composed of the familiar stucco, metal, and glass of the existing auditorium building. Because the visual environment is especially important to the hearing-impaired, the design makes full use of form, color, and light inside and out.

2

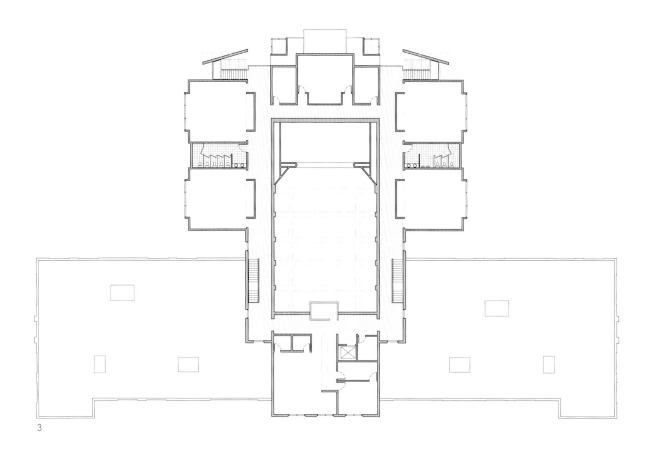

3

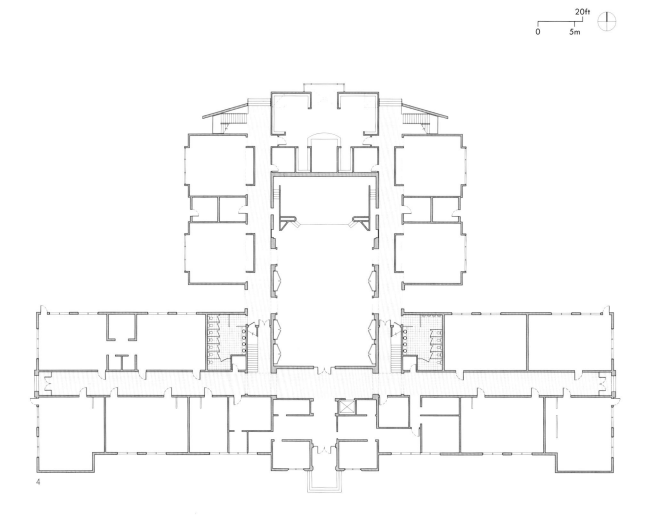

4

3 Upper level plan
4 Ground level plan
5 Night view

Bringing Discipline to Design

Building quality architecture requires the right balance between thoughtful design sensibilities and solid management skills. Both are key components of successful project outcomes.

When Ronald Altoon and I started the firm, we prioritized both the design and technical aspects of architecture, combined with strong systems of management. This model has served us well, as we have grown from a local firm working on regional projects to an international firm with a global reach. We continue to maintain solid business practices that mirror the way that our clients themselves operate on a daily basis.

Discipline and craft are values that inform our design methodology, as well as our approach to project management. They are also qualities that resonate personally with me. As a big band musician prior to beginning my career in architecture, I gained an early and profound appreciation of the need for concentration, attention to detail, and the ability to work in unison with my professional peers.

Architecture, too, is like a score of music which requires precision and focus to ensure that the final product sings. All participants on a project—from the architects to the client and consultants—have to hit the right notes.

Our firm was founded on a similar spirit of collaboration. In addition to the partners' hands-on duties for specific projects, each of us has undertaken a special role within the firm. To maintain consistency in our work and ensure design excellence, the individual partners are responsible for a specific aspect of the practice, such as project administration, information technology, technical services, and global design. This method of focused oversight provides a navigational tool from start to finish.

Such an approach has enabled us to provide the level of quality that clients have come to expect and to promote an exchange of ideas among professional staff. Teamwork is not just a buzzword; it is an integral part of the way that we conduct the business of design. Establishing flexibility as a practice of project management has resulted in greater innovation in our portfolio and more creative solutions as a whole.

As we have expanded our practice overseas, we have continued to share our body of knowledge with partner firms. Diversification and growth have provided us with many opportunities to collaborate with architects throughout the world, often on complex projects of a grand scale.

Over the past two decades, we have constantly reviewed and refined our methods to meet the needs of expanding markets and the dynamic character of our business. In more recent years, we introduced a matrix that defines the division of responsibility for two architecture firms so that we can practice efficiently and effectively as an alliance of equals, with respective but unique capabilities. Clients get the personalized attention they desire and a quick response to issues that inevitably arise during the design and construction of projects.

These methods have enabled us to expand our reach around the globe as we continue to pursue distinctive projects that bring fresh design challenges and yield unexpected and gratifying rewards for our clients and ourselves.

James F. Porter, AIA
Partner

CLIMATE AND TERRAIN

The natural elements present challenge and opportunity in equal measure. The projects of Altoon + Porter Architects not only respond to the rigors of a steep hillside site or the unrelenting heat of the desert, but also exploit these qualities to create architecture that is uniquely of its environment. Harsh or gentle, these forces require the architects to find elegant and inventive solutions that will work in harmony with them. Meeting the demands of climate and terrain has also taught the firm to practice a truly sustainable design that now informs all of its work.

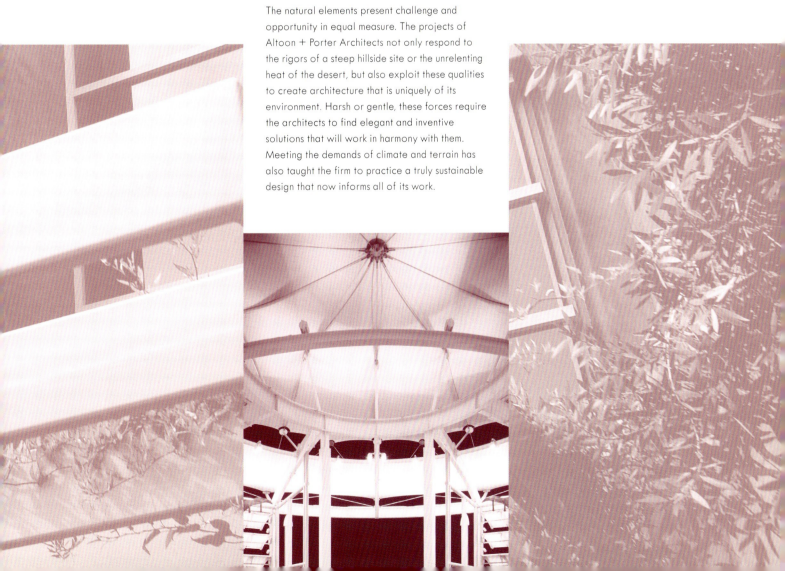

1 Canopy detail
2 Structural detail
3 Iconic entry canopy

Design 1990/Completion 1994

Maui, Land & Pineapple Company, Inc.

600,000 square feet

Steel structure, eifs, metal panels, Teflon-coated fiberglass roof, concrete interlocking pavers

Ka'ahumanu Center
Maui, Hawaii

The imagery and function of Ka'ahumanu Center capture the essence of Maui's natural climate and landscape. High technology and indigenous architectural features are ingeniuously combined in an improved retail environment. An open structural system conserves and forges a connection with the island's striking physical beauty.

The expansion created generous interior spaces and a bolder, up-to-date image. Above a new second floor, an undulating roof floats atop a delicate steel frame. Multiple layers of Teflon-coated fiberglass form a lightweight roof canopy that is supported by tension wires. This permanent and permeable structure allows air and light to circulate and shields shoppers from heat and rain. The roofline's lofty surface terminates at a luminous skylight. Along the sides, the canopy's taut surface dissolves into a series of flat panels that swing open and closed like the billowing sails of trade ships powered by the Kona winds. Openings between the panels reveal views of the surrounding sea, sky, and mountains.

Sleek, supple surfaces are balanced by references to the native culture of Maui. Paving patterns imitate the play of light on the ocean, and custom-designed light fixtures, illuminated at night, evoke the torches of island villages. Architectural details and signage incorporate local flora and a likeness of the 19th-century Queen Ka'ahumanu. Outdoor and indoor landscaping celebrates the island's varied and exotic plants.

4 Site plan
5 View to entrance from food court

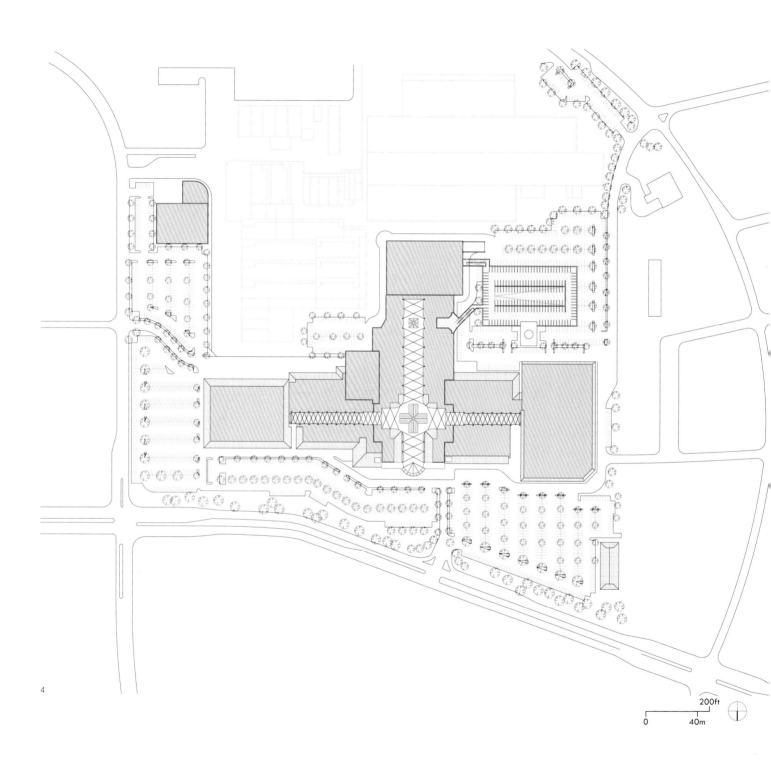

4

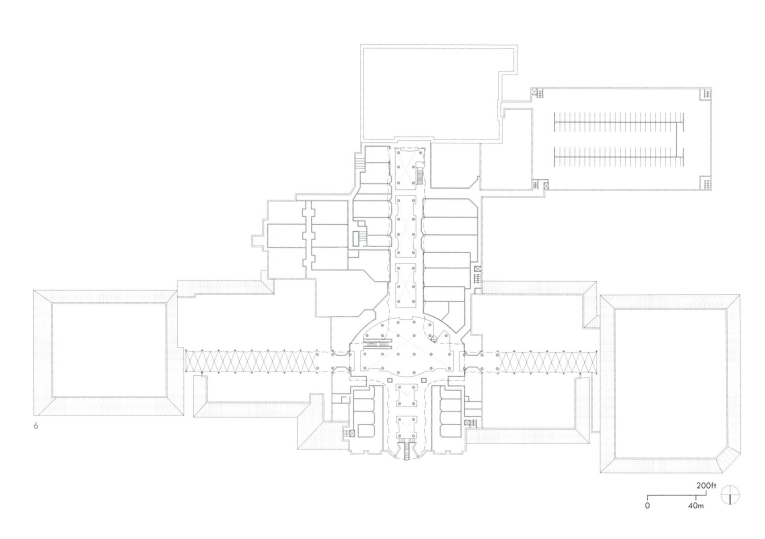

6

7

6 Site plan
7 Central court
8 Illuminated entry
9 Canopy detail
10 Perspective
11 View to mountainscape

8

9

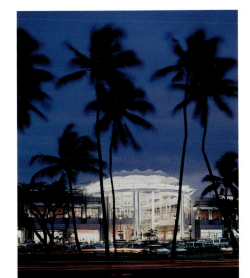
10

11

1 Site plan
2 Tower detail
3 Viewing tower
4 View toward mountains
5 Historic petroglyphs

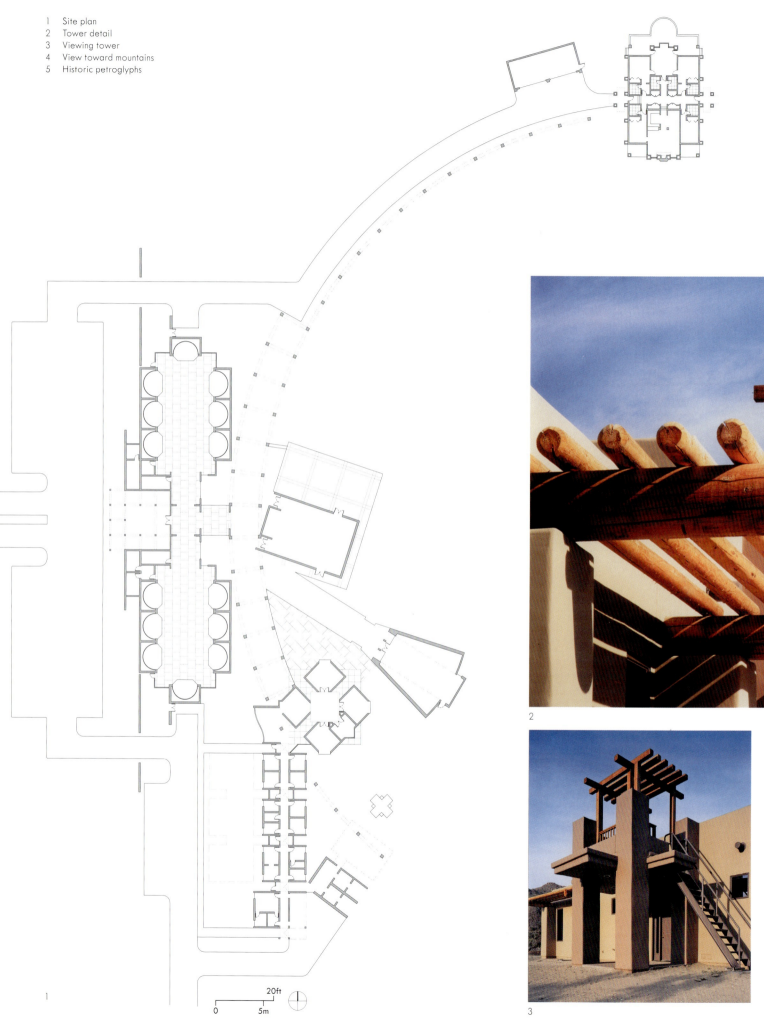

Design 1993/Completion 1995
Bighorn Institute
20,000 square feet
Wood-framed structure, cement plaster exterior, wood trellis

BIGHORN INSTITUTE
PALM DESERT, CALIFORNIA

Bighorn Institute is a research center for the only American organization that is licensed to care for bighorn sheep. Acting as a sanctuary for animal care and a headquarters for public outreach, the Institute comprises a hospital and study laboratory, a residential facility for on-site scientists, and a public museum that creates greater awareness about the plight of the sheep population whose mortality rate is as high as 97 percent.

The Institute is based on the Middle Eastern model of the caravanserai, a walled compound that traditionally provided shelter for travelers crossing the desert. The low-scale stucco buildings create a distinctive visual complex that reflects the shapes and colors of the desert environment and surrounding mountains. The secluded nature of the Institute provides privacy for the resident scientists and their work.

The buildings protect the fragile desert environment of California in which they are located. The thick walls, high ceilings, and clerestory windows of the buildings conserve energy by providing natural ventilation and diffused lighting that mitigates the impact of the arid climate. The public museum is isolated from the scientists and the sheep, while allowing visitors to experience the important work of the Institute.

1

1 Sculpture gardens
2 Palm bosque and fountain
3 Trellis detail
4 Paseo

Design 1994/Completion 1998

Madison Realty Partnership

209,000 square feet

Steel structure, cement plaster, interlocking pavers, wood trellis, concrete

THE GARDENS ON EL PASEO
PALM DESERT, CALIFORNIA

The Gardens on El Paseo, a 209,000-square-foot open-air complex combines retail facilities and pedestrian amenities, reinforcing the resort character of Palm Desert. Conceived as an urban village center, the project creates an architectural landmark along Palm Desert's premier shopping corridor. The Gardens include a 50,000-square-foot resort specialty store, 110,000 square feet of shops, and 50,000 square feet of upscale restaurants.

Designed as a formal composition of buildings, paseos, nodes, and civic spaces, the two-level buildings along El Paseo embrace urban and natural environments. The simple architectural forms are shaped from indigenous materials, such as stucco and stone. Rich earth colors predominate, ranging from terra cotta to sage. At the center of the site, the buildings converge on a spacious and richly landscaped plaza. Cafés, galleries, and outdoor restaurants that are located on recessed second-floor terraces allow outdoor diners and shoppers to survey the plaza activity from above.

Traditional methods of planning and building design mitigate the harsh desert temperatures and create climatic comfort levels that are in harmony with social usage. The buildings are interspersed with desert gardens and tranquil paseos filled with native plants, palm trees, and fountains. High, narrow passages induce a gentle upward breeze. Curved wooden trellises balance the solid buildings and give a quiet sense of formal order to the gardens that are framed by views of the Santa Rosa mountains and the California sky.

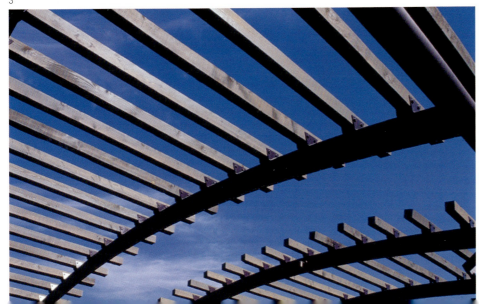

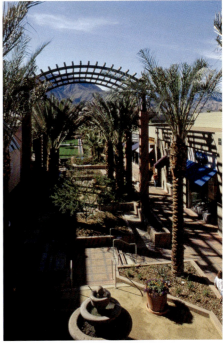

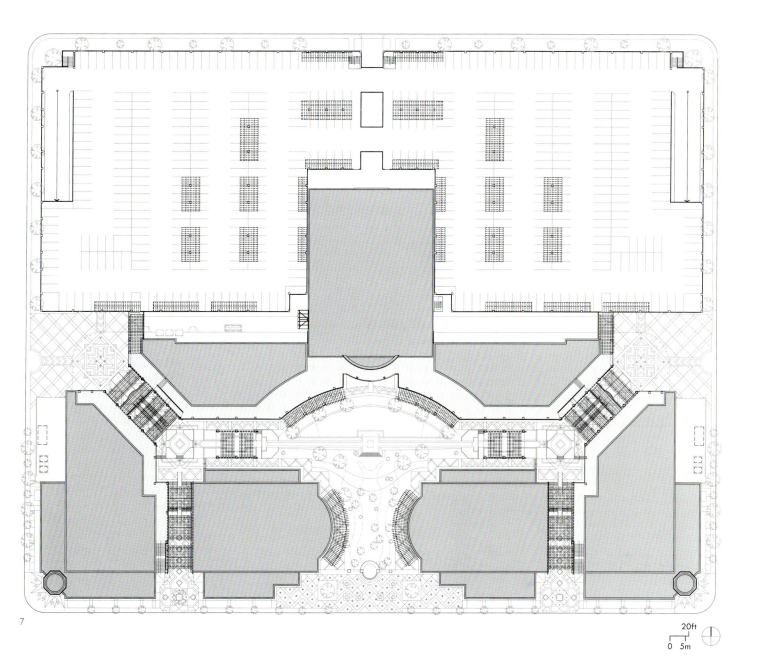

7

8

5 Entry paseo
6 Central courtyard
7 Site plan
8 Paseo

Design 1995/Completion 1998

AMP Henderson Global Investors

1,197,943 square feet

Steel and glass canopies, tensile fabric roofs, natural stone, limestone, sandstone, masonry, concrete, plaster

WARRINGAH MALL
SYDNEY, NEW SOUTH WALES, AUSTRALIA

The renovation and expansion of Warringah Mall in northern Sydney reinstated in the retail facility a visual clarity that had been lost over time. The new design captures the beachside ambiance of the 16-hectare site, while adding two new spaces: an interior room and exterior place for public gatherings as well as 133 additional tenant spaces for a total of 272 shops.

The project turns the rules of retail upside down in the "land down under." The use of unexpected iconography and the center's flexible design reflect the project's location at the confluence of three ecological zones—hillside, valley, and beachfront. This diversity of climatic conditions generated a complex that is equally diverse in its architecture, ranging from enclosed and semi-enclosed spaces to a retail wing that was left completely open to the air. Trellises, arcades, skylights, and translucent fabric roof systems enhance the experience by maximizing natural light and connections to the landscape.

The once disparate retail spaces were organized into a series of neighborhoods that respond to the casual lifestyle of the Northern Beaches. An inviting open-air court creates a communal, civic space at the center of the mall. Glass-covered spines connect the courtyard with the various neighborhoods and orient visitors as they move throughout the complex.

1 Canopy profile
2 Trellis arch
3 Outdoor court
4 Environmental graphic detail

2

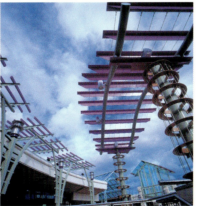

3

4

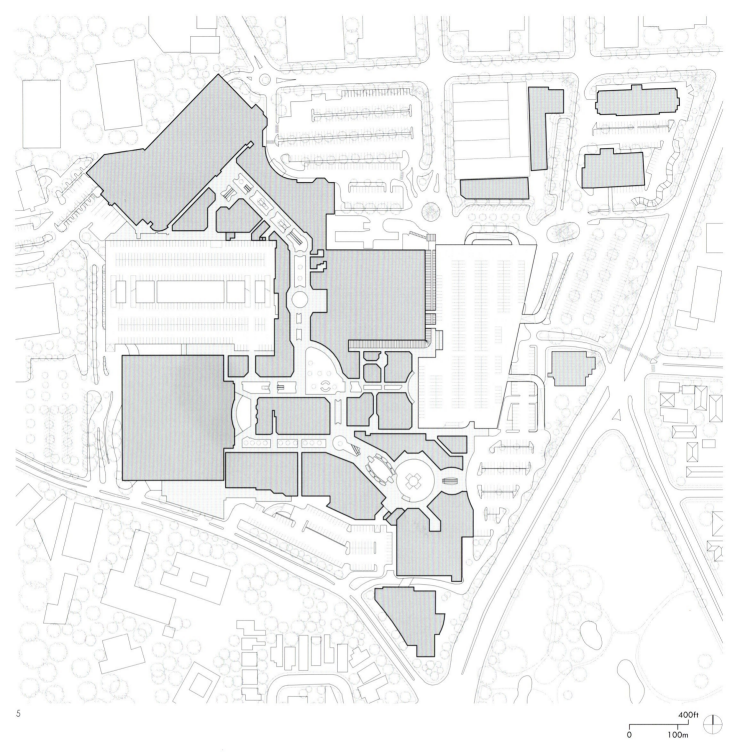

5

6

7

5 Site plan
6 Stone detail
7 Art glass panel
8 Retail passage
9 Interior court
10 Graphics
11 Custom lighting
12 Indoor detail

8

9

10

11

12

Warringah Mall 85

1
2   3   4

Design 2000/Completion 2005

Porter Development

West Residence: 6425 square feet; South Residence: 5630 square feet;
North Residence: 6590 square feet; East Residence: 8650 square feet

Natural stone, stucco, metal and wood trellis and lattice work, aluminum windows, metal roofing

Carrara Place Compound
Los Angeles, California

On a steep hillside in the Brentwood Hills, these three contemporary residences were designed to maximize the tight site and capitalize on the canyon and city views. The programs for the four-bedroom homes are carefully laid out on three floors to provide multiple opportunities for decks, terraces, double-height rooms and large windows.

Bends and twists in the design tuck the components of the buildings into the landscape to achieve the quiet intimacy and privacy of a house on a hill on one side, and a generosity of light and vista on the other. The modernist aesthetic is achieved by strong geometric forms and the use of stucco, metal, and glass. Stonework detail and plantings on applied trellises further tie the buildings into the surrounding topography. Each property has its own distinctive roofline—curved, angular and butterfly—that provides visual interest and individuality.

The residences complete an architectural composition of six homes in the canyon. The careful siting and design allows each residence to enjoy a sense of privacy as well as the luxury of Southern California's indoor/outdoor lifestyle.

1   Approach from drive
2   Illuminated view
3   Entry court
4   Corner detail
5   Entrance

Opposite View to interior stair
7 Main façade

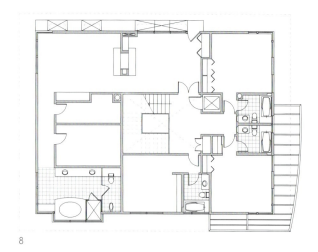

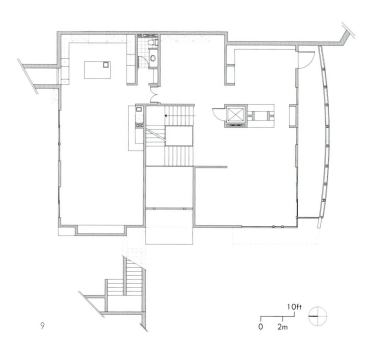

8 Third floor plan
9 Main living floor plan
10 Atrium stair
11 Stairway
12 Living area
13 View from entrance court
14 Entrance walkway
15 Living room

13

14

15

Carrara Place Compound: South Residence 91

16

16　View from bottom of hill
17　Mid-level floor plan – master suite
18　Main entry level floor plan
19　Main living area
20　Mountain view

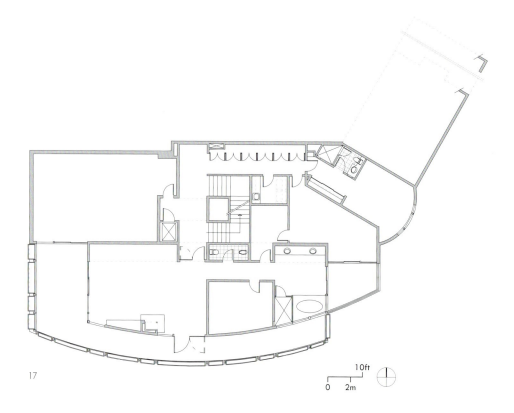

17

18

19

20

Carrara Place Compound: East Residence 93

21

22

23

21 View from driveway
22 Entrance
23 Main living area
24 Main living level floor plan
25 Second level detail

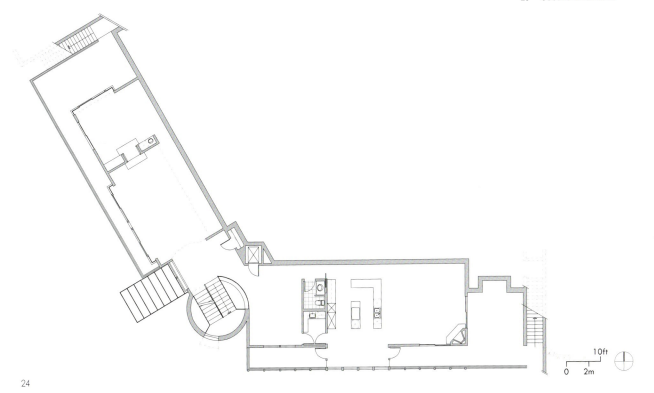

27

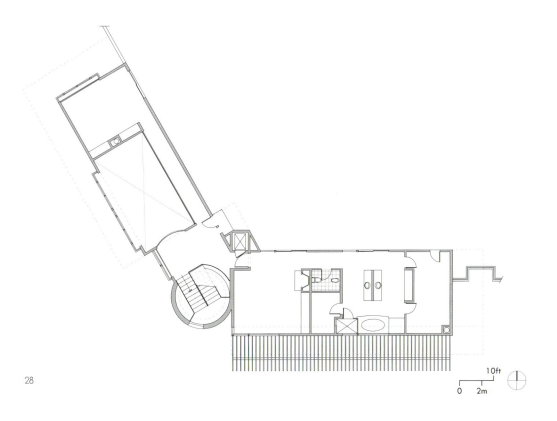

28

Opposite Main façade
27 Illuminated view
28 Third floor plan

Carrara Place Compound: North Residence   97

1

2

3

4

Design 2002/Completion 2007

American University of Armenia

10,000-square-meter, 5-story classroom building

Honed and rustic tuffa stone, basalt stone, glass curtainwall

Paramaz Avedisian Building
American University of Armenia
Yerevan, Armenia

In Yerevan, the ancient capital of Armenia, on a hill facing Mount Ararat, the tallest mountain in the country's historic homeland, the American University of Armenia is adding a state-of-the-art academic building complex to expand its single-structure campus. The building is set into a steep hillside site in a precarious seismic zone. The harsh climate, unpredictable energy grid, onerous building codes, a tight budget, and limited access to materials and skilled constructors would challenge even a simple project. The University required an innovative, flexible building that would provide classrooms for students, offices for faculty and administrative staff, and a residence for the president of the university.

Adapting the complex program to the constraints of a 10,000-square-meter building required an in-depth utilization study and a design that takes full advantage of modular solutions that allow the spaces to serve multiple purposes. To meet demand for advanced, highly flexible technology, the building is designed to accommodate the latest in video, computer, and telecommunications equipment, including wireless networking.

The design is an environmentally sensitive solution that creates alternative solutions to the university's energy needs. These include simple concepts such as setting the building orientation to minimize heat gain in the summer and maximize light in the winter; sophisticated innovations that include a thermal flue that captures heat in winter and induces cooling in summer; a breathing stone wall that adds additional insulation; and light shelves that reflect low winter sun deep into the south-facing rooms. A solar farm provides energy year-round and energy-recycling wheels capture and re-use expended energy.

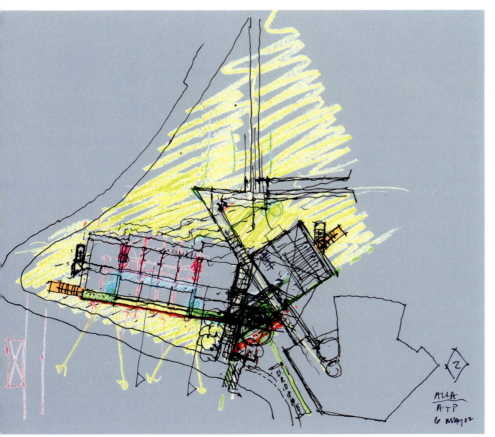

1&2 Computer rendering
3 Model
4 Perspective drawing
5 Concept sketch

5

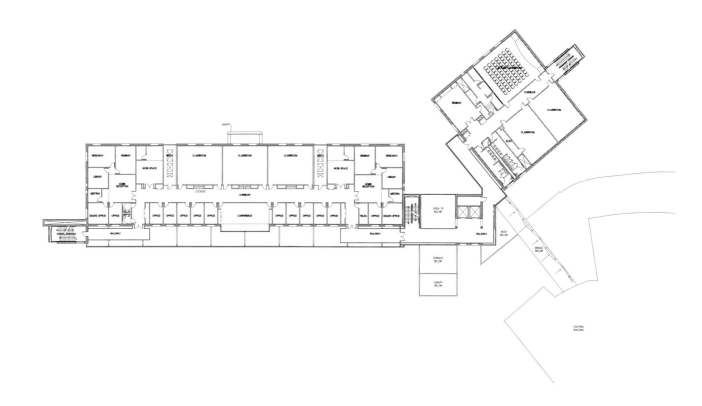

6

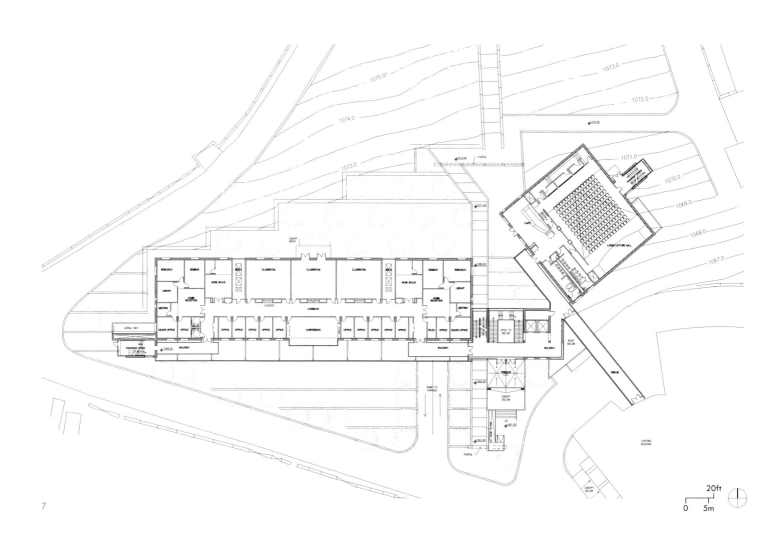

7

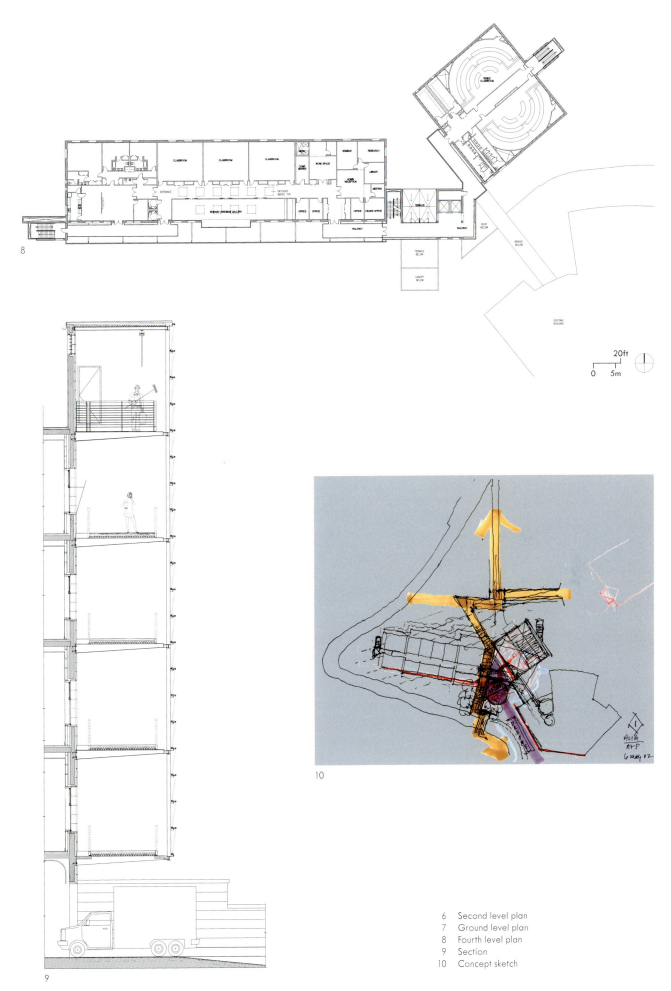

6   Second level plan
7   Ground level plan
8   Fourth level plan
9   Section
10 Concept sketch

Paramaz Avedisian Building

1 Southeast bird's-eye view
2 Southeast view
3 Southwest view
4 Northwest view
5 Northeast view

Design 2004/Completion 2007

Ventura County Community College District

13,000 square feet

Concrete masonry unit, glass, metal roofing

Exotic Animal Training and Management Facility, Moorpark College
Ventura, California

The Exotic Animal Training and Management Program at Moorpark College is nationally recognized as America's teaching zoo. This unusual program has attracted attention and students from all over the world, prompting the Trustees of the Ventura County Community College to expand the facilities.

The site, on a hillside at the eastern edge of the college campus, will accommodate complex program requirements including classrooms, labs, offices for faculty and staff, as well as indoor and outdoor dining, a gift/bookstore, a reception lobby and ticket room that must be accessible to the public and readily secured. Further, the college wanted to take advantage of views offered by the steeply sloped site for public functions and, at the same time, to provide discrete access for educational use, including the transport of animals on a lower level.

The architectural design responds to program demands and to the image-building/outreach goals for the EATM program, the zoo, the site and Moorpark College. Massed as two separate buildings connected by a broad terrace, the simple plan maximizes the opportunities of the hillside setting for visibility and for vertical circulation. Architecturally the building reflects the clean, modernist design standards of the campus with the exception of the graceful, curvilinear roofs that echo the forms of the rolling hills and establish a signature presence for the renowned program.

3

4   5

8

6 Lower level plan
7 Upper level plan
8 Site plan

Exotic Animal Training and Management 105
Facility, Moorpark College

COLLABORATION AND CONSTRUCTION

I have been practicing architecture for 28 years, 26 of those with my partners Ronald Altoon, James Porter, and William Sebring. One of the things that has made me proud of our relationship is that we build buildings together. We design our projects to be constructed.

The construction process is the ultimate collaborative effort in architecture. Individuals and companies, with varied backgrounds, experiences and expectations, are brought together by the client to construct his building. A critical task for the architect is to "captain" this team. It can be daunting to convince people you have just met to believe in something that only exists in your imagination.

Your drawings reflect what you believe they will need to know about this building that has never been built before. You make assumptions regarding what information is of the highest priority to document with the belief that the rest is self-evident or will evolve during the course of construction. Other members of the team price, and sometimes guarantee that price, based on your documentation. With this interaction the construction process begins

Maintaining a collaborative process requires sensitivity. The architect must understand the contributions as well as the concerns and expectations of all the team members. This willingness to listen and understand multiple points of view seems obvious, but is all too uncommon.

In the field the design process requires the same collaborative effort as it does in the office—it just involves additional parties. As a design practice, we always benefit from the advice of the masons, tile setters, electricians and other tradespeople regarding solutions to problems. While it is unconventional, we include the trades in the process. Without exception it encourages their contribution, their ownership of the building, and improves the process. Including subcontractors in site meetings and key team meetings with the client is also key to collaboration. Then when there is the inevitable disagreement, the resolution is based on what is good for the project, not who was to blame. The result: better buildings and better relationships.

Architects are not always perfect and that is sometimes true of our drawings. Other team members are human too. What works best in the construction process is individual responsibility. Rather than spending time and energy on documenting mistakes, we prefer to engage in the solution

Our clients hire us to deliver their buildings and they expect that we will work with teams of professionals to accomplish that. The design team must be prepared to solve the problems that the construction team faces. Collaboration leads to success, to satisfied clients, to a motivated team and to a very personal fulfillment in our work.

Gary K. Dempster, AIA
Partner

TECHNOLOGY

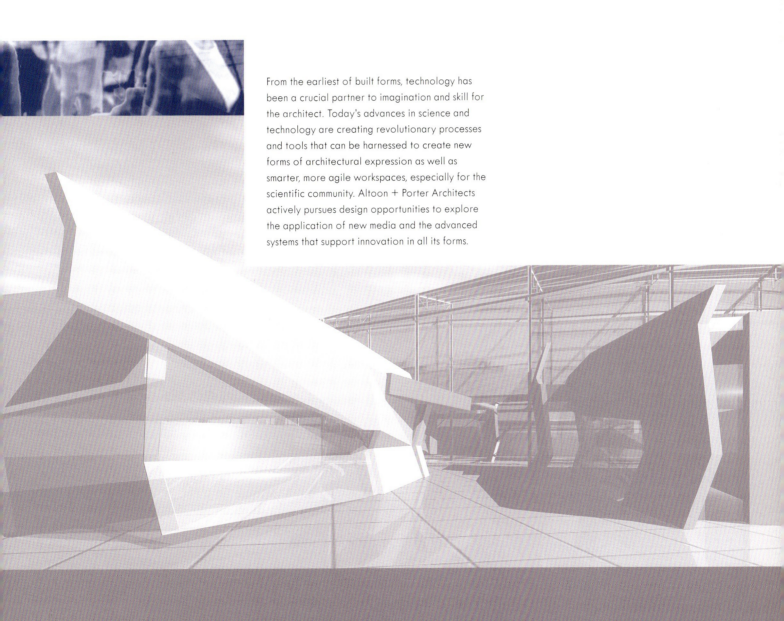

From the earliest of built forms, technology has been a crucial partner to imagination and skill for the architect. Today's advances in science and technology are creating revolutionary processes and tools that can be harnessed to create new forms of architectural expression as well as smarter, more agile workspaces, especially for the scientific community. Altoon + Porter Architects actively pursues design opportunities to explore the application of new media and the advanced systems that support innovation in all its forms.

1 Plaza
2 View from the Las Vegas Strip
3 Street entryway
4 View toward "The Cloud"
5 LED screens on the plaza

1

2

3

Design 1999/Completion 2003

The Rouse Company

1,785,000 square feet, including 72,000-square-foot plaza, and a 600-foot-long by 185-foot-tall "cloud"

Steel structure, metal panel, glass curtainwall, limestone, perforated metal

Fashion Show
Las Vegas, Nevada

Doubling the size of the 1-million-square-foot Fashion Show transformed it from a regional mall into a lifestyle destination for international visitors along the Las Vegas Strip. The expansion added three department stores and numerous upscale retail boutiques in an airy, long-span structure.

The indoor areas are organized around a great hall with projecting balconies, soaring columns, and a linear runway that emerges hydraulically from the floor to capture the dynamic nature of fashion shows. Permanent rigging for lighting drops from the slotted ceiling above and an audio-visual studio on a balcony assures proper transmission of the fashion shows throughout the galleries and to the huge screens outdoors on the Strip.

Outdoors, a large, high-tech overhead structure known as "The Cloud" is suspended from two 200-foot-high box-trusses by tension cables. It creates a bold image in the context of the iconic buildings that define the Las Vegas Strip. Suspended 180 feet in the air, the structure provides shade for an outdoor plaza and is capable of lowering the hot desert temperature by 15 degrees Fahrenheit. This open-air plaza is a gathering place where visitors watch fashion shows in real time.

Moving images are projected against The Cloud and on the building itself by a series of four enormous 24-foot by 42-foot LED screens that move on tracks. The sophisticated and flexible audio-visual system can modify the appearance of the retail center with a rapidity that matches the changes in current fashion trends.

4

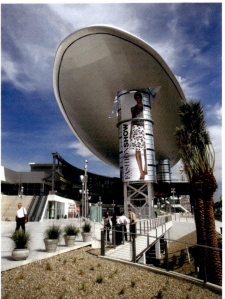

5

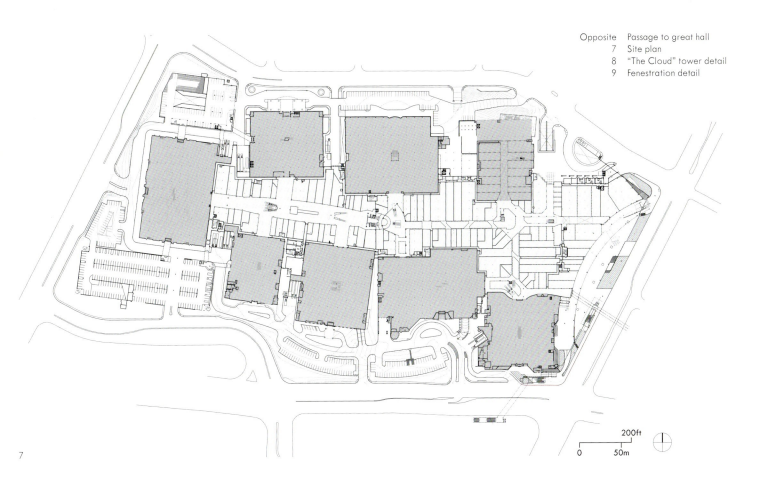

Opposite Passage to great hall
7 Site plan
8 "The Cloud" tower detail
9 Fenestration detail

10

10 Plaza illuminated
11 Two-level storefront
12 Kiosks
13 Catwalk and control booth
14 View of great hall

11

12

13

14

Fashion Show 115

1 South elevation
2 Detail of stone façade
3 View of main entrance
4 View into plaza axis
5 Main entrance elevation

Design 2001/Completion 2006

University of California, Santa Barbara

110,000 gross square feet

Formed concrete structure, European limestone with granite, sandstone and marble accents,
precast concrete, storefront glazing

UCSB California NanoSystems Institute
Santa Barbara, California

The 110,000-square-foot California NanoSystems Institute Laboratory contains a variety of innovative laboratory spaces that support collaborative, cutting-edge research in the nanosciences at University of California, Santa Barbara. A café and a 600-car parking garage are included in the plan. Located at the east entrance to the campus, the massing of the Institute pulls the east–west axis from the Campus Green through the site, highlighting views of the ocean.

The Institute and the parking structure face each other across a courtyard that symbolizes the shared nature of research and creates a place for community. The lobby is located at the juncture of the two buildings. A colonnade wraps around the courtyard, joining the two volumes. The façades have limestone and precast concrete surfaces, and the east façade doubles as a screen for projected images. A café is located on the ground floor of the parking structure.

The state-of-the-art facilities contain modular laboratories, life sciences laboratories, a fully immersive presentation space, and other research spaces for the study of nanosystems, spectroscopy, and imaging. They also include the University's progressive Media Arts and Technology and Performance departments, conference rooms, and faculty offices. The project was designed in association with Venturi, Scott Brown & Associates.

5

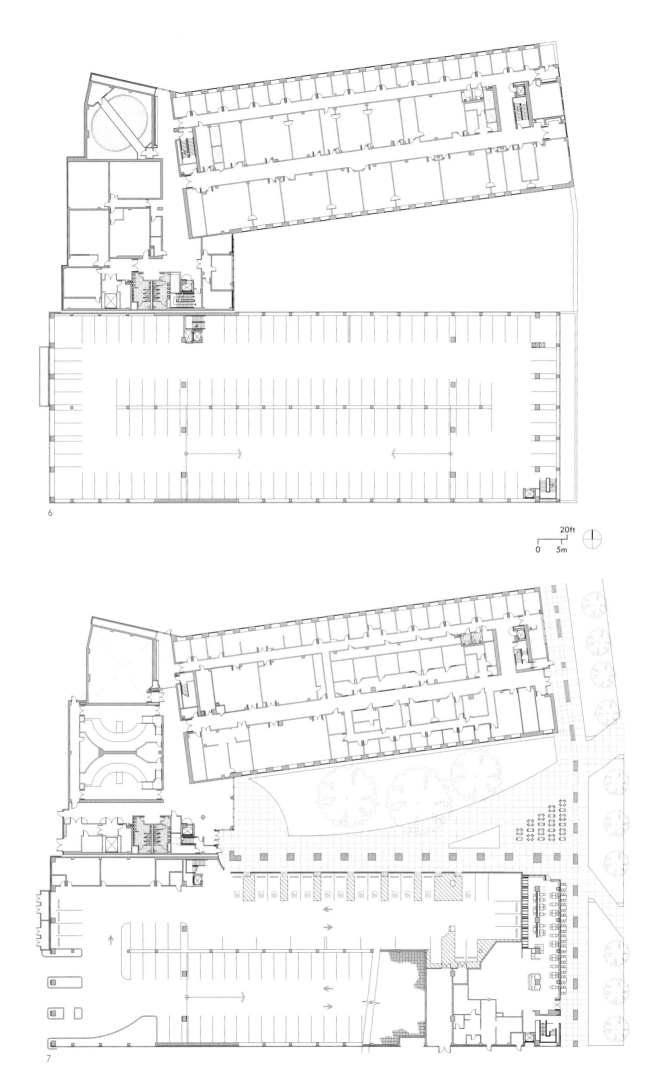

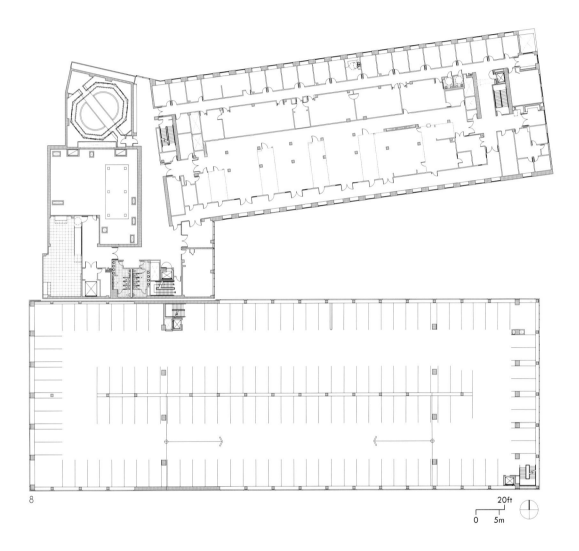

6 Second level plan
7 Ground level plan
8 Third level plan

1 City context – site plan
2 Illuminated main façade
3 Ground level plan

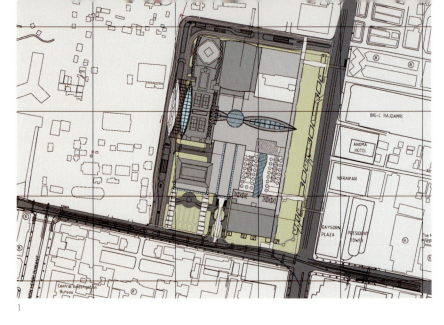

Design 2003/Completion 2006

Central Pattana Property Investment & Development

220,000 square meters

Glass, radiused metal panels, stainless steel cable truss and spider connection, stainless steel fabric, granite, terrazzo

Central World Plaza
Bangkok, Thailand

Central World Plaza, with its large outdoor space, is the civic heart of Bangkok's main shopping district, the Thai capital's Times Square. The project is being redeveloped to be more competitive as a mixed-use center that will include a wide range of uses and experiences and will bring the excitement of the annual New Year's Eve countdown to the location all year round. Visually, the most exciting new addition is a phenomenal seven-story-high, 350-meter-long digital Media Wall, with the capability to project multiple LED images, tickertape and lasers. The new high-tech face of the greatly expanded center looks out on a revitalized plaza complete with fountains and gardens.

Among the new offerings that will flash across the big screen are a variety of retail "rooms" or precincts, an Olympic ice rink, bowling, a fitness center, a convention center, high-rise hotel, 50-story office space, and multiple entertainment spots. The redesign of the retail center transforms the existing eight-story maze by opening up the plan and moving the vertical circulation including stairs, escalators, and elevators to the interstitial space between the wall of the building and the media screen, which hangs from the existing façade.

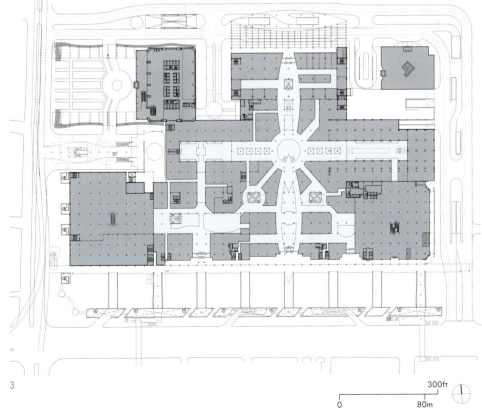

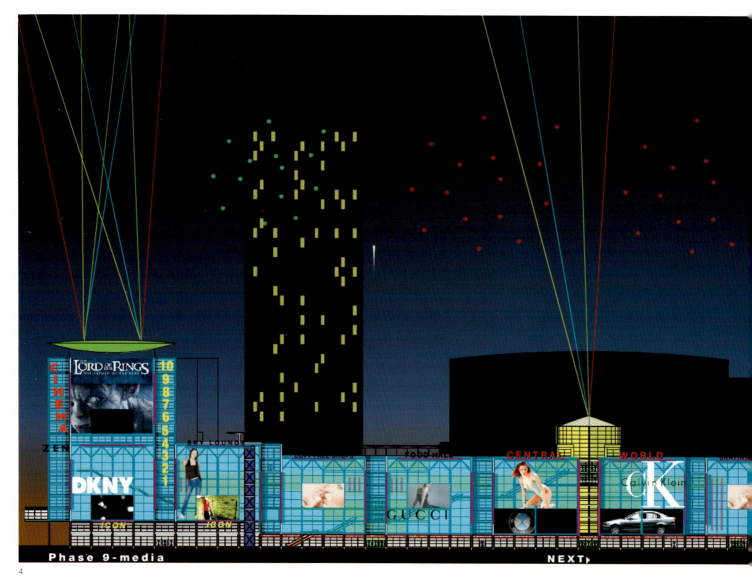

4

4   Plaza elevation
5   Fashion court
6   Center atrium

5

6

Central World Plaza 123

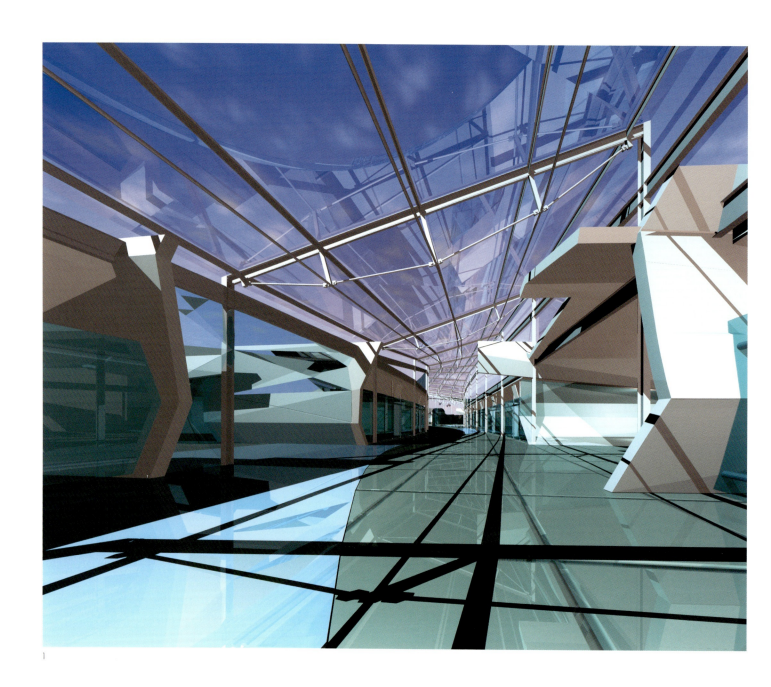

1 Retail passageway
2 Entry

Design 2001

Auchan Ipermercati Grouppo Rinascente, sponsored by L'Arca

63,000 square meters

Glass skylight supported by pin-mounted stainless steel connectors, contemporary steel and tension cable trusses, precast concrete, brushed stainless steel, cast aluminum

Auchan Competition
Suburban site, Italy

This 63,000-square-meter complex was designed as a prototype for hypermarket stores that would create a civic presence and create a sense of community for the customers in the regions they served. The international design competition, conducted by Auchan, a large and successful Italian retailer, explores the development of a model hypermarket and retail center for its suburban markets.

The design was based on the two different kinds of movement that define the retail experience: passage within the store itself, and passage to and from the building. These separate activities are reflected in two distinct vocabularies of space and form.

In order to encourage movement through the building, the retail center was designed as a linear composition with a central, glazed seam that emphasizes continuous, dynamic passage along its transverse spine. This long space is interrupted by five gaps that fracture the exterior shell of the building, creating spontaneous points of entry and egress. Unlike the typical retail center that is isolated from the outdoors, this prototype enhances the ebbs and flows that characterize the pedestrian experience.

3 Plan
4 Elevation
5 Aerial view
6 Passageway

4

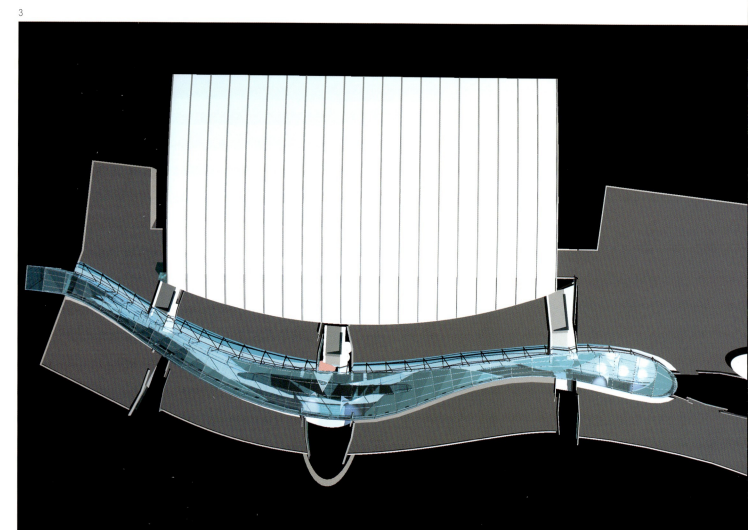
3

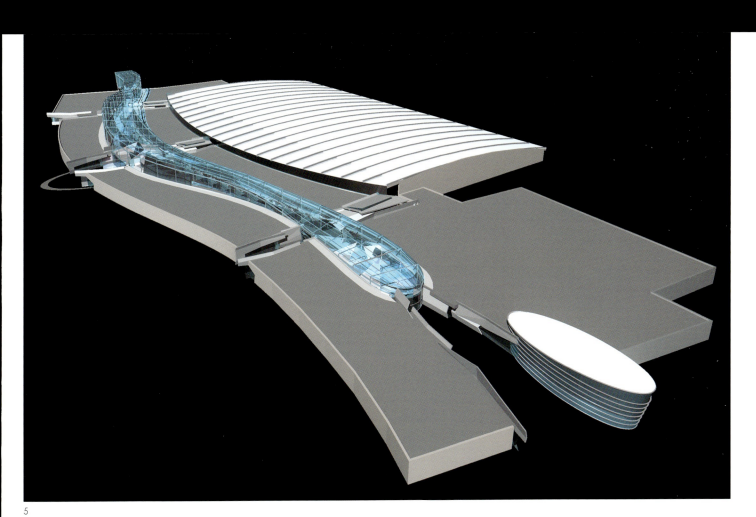

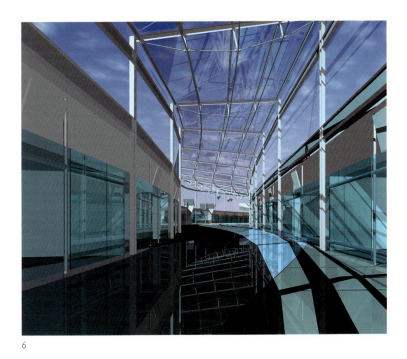

1 Aerial perspective
2 Entry court
3 Site plan

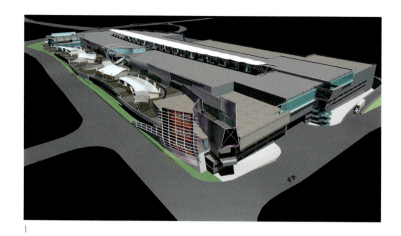

1

2

Design 2001

Filo S.A.

60,000 square meters

Tensile Teflon-coated fiberglass system, local natural stone and concrete, glass, stainless steel, precast concrete panels, pinned lattice elements of steel framing

SetúCentre
Setúbal, Portugal

The scheme for this shopping center plays on the themes of adventure and travel that define Setúbal, a seafront town that was an historic point of demarcation for 15th-century explorers. Designed for an international competition, the 60,000-square-meter retail complex is anchored by a large hypermarket with ample outdoor spaces. A retail mall is perpendicular to the hypermarket and enables a wide display of merchandise along a central spine, as well as convenient access to parking.

The interaction between the major components of the project adds a sense of discovery to the retail environment that encourages socializing. The hypermarket serves as an attraction that draws in customers, while the elongated retail corridor takes the form of an indoor bazaar that allows for more casual shopping experiences.

The mall is extended to the outdoors where a series of pavilions establish a public precinct that opens onto the surrounding streets. The public space is sited to benefit from the cooling sea breezes that filter through the Mediterranean town. The combination of indoor and outdoor spaces creates a civic realm that transforms the typical hypermarket experience from a daily chore to a place where customers can congregate, dine, and relax.

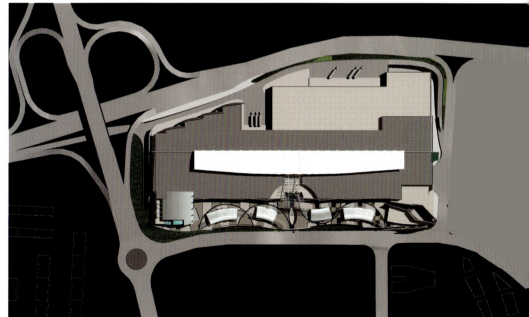

3

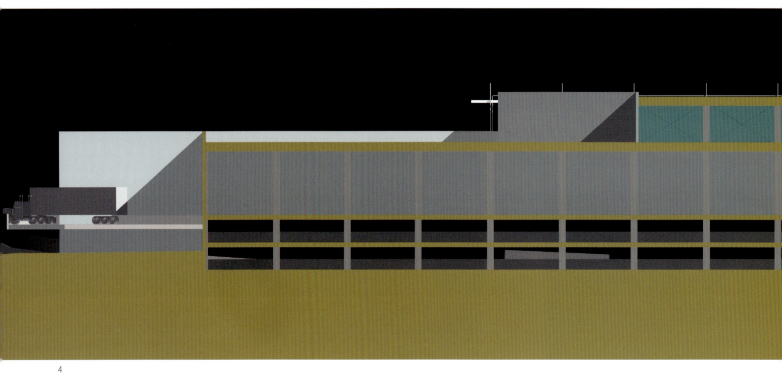

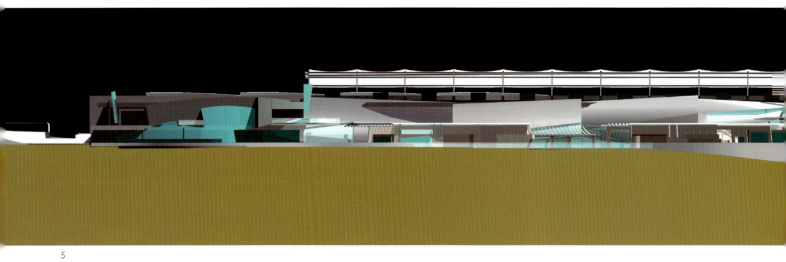

4 Section
5 South elevation

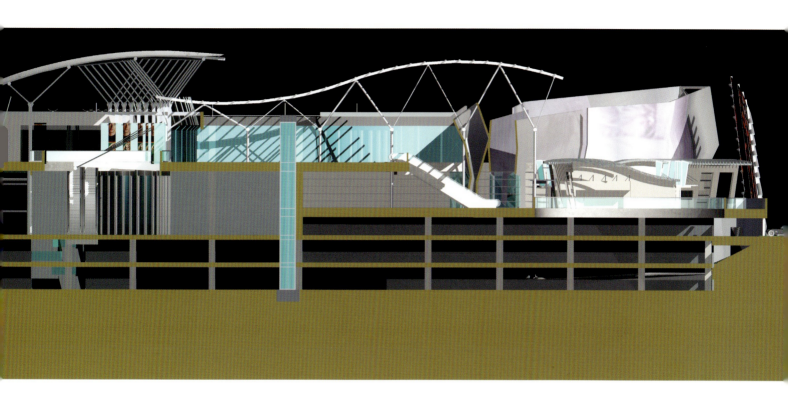
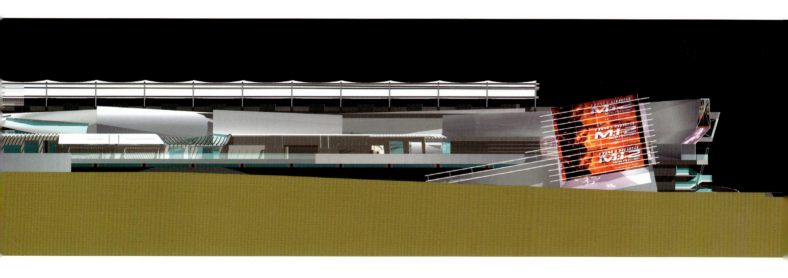

SetúCentre 131

1 View to transit connection
2 Roof garden

Design 2001

Rodamco Ceska Republika

64,000 square meters

Mega-scaled stone and glass panels, backlit colored graphics, traditional concrete block and plaster systems, contemporary wood/polymer composite planks

CHODOV CENTRUM
PRAGUE, CZECH REPUBLIC

Located in a satellite community outside of Prague, this 64,000-square-meter shopping center is the first phase of a new town center. The project adds needed public services to a Soviet-era housing complex that was never fully completed. Civic, retail, and residential spaces establish a sense of community for residents of the housing complex. As a symbol of the political and social changes that have occurred in the past decade, the development reaffirms the country's successful transition from communism to democracy.

The four-story retail center has an organic plan that balances the rigid architectural forms of the residential structures. The retail program forms a new circulation system that reinforces the pedestrian realm. A mix of stores and public amenities for residents of Chodov are organized around open spaces for shopping and socializing. The base of the building is linked to a transit concourse for the subway system that is lined by public amenities. The roof has a large garden, a dining facility, and a cinema and creates an elevated platform that affords panoramic views of the surrounding countryside.

2

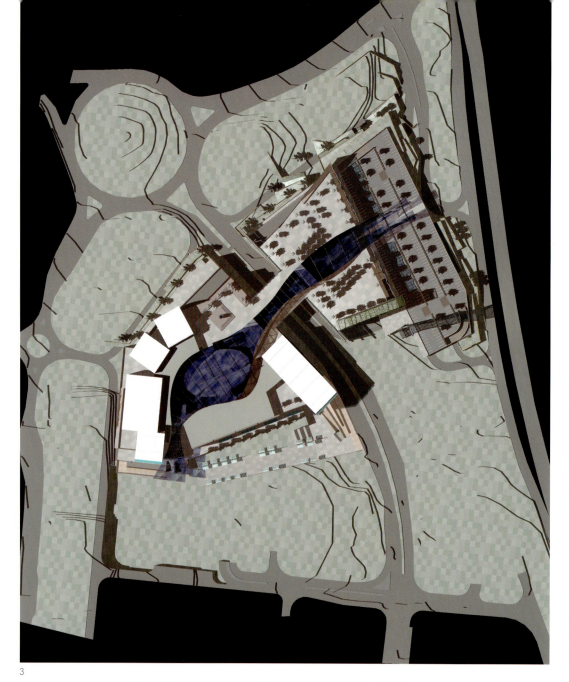

3

4

5

3 Site plan
4 East elevation
5 North elevation

Chodov Centrum 135

COMMUNITY

Civic architecture is a powerful antidote to social isolation and fragmentation. For Altoon + Porter Architects, civic buildings are not necessarily grand public edifices but rather the mix of residences, schools, shops, and public squares that provide ordinary people with the quality of life, especially public life, that fosters caring and engagement. Wherever the firm works, the buildings are designed with the same quality, presence, and vitality because the designers believe that architecture is the foundation of strong communities.

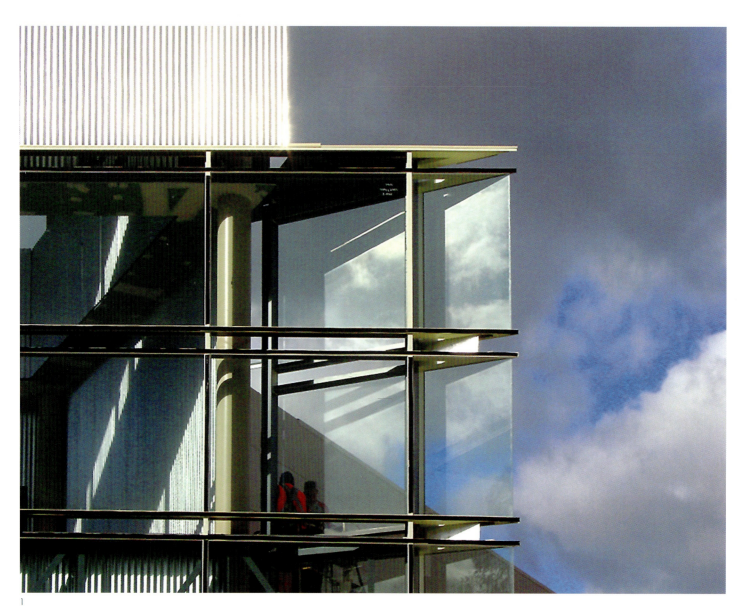

1

2

1 Window detail
2 Ceiling detail
3 Protective overhangs
4 Canopy detail

Design 1997/Completion 2003

AMP Henderson Global Investors

1,450,000 square feet

Steel, glass, polished wood, perforated metal, frameless glass, Teflon-coated fabric canopies, local natural polished stone, basalt, travertine, brick pavers, cobblestone, smooth-trowelled painted cement, galvanized steel sheeting, timber columns, timber structure

Knox City Centre
Melbourne, Victoria, Australia

Knox City Centre is the first phase of a long-range master plan to create an urban framework for a 21st-century neighborhood on the outskirts of Melbourne. Patterned after the city plan for Savannah, Georgia, the project includes 1,450,000 square feet of retail, office, civic, and residential buildings that reshape a regional retail center into a robust community that is connected to the area's culture and history. The center offers a variety of leisure options in a comfortable setting that reflects the diversity of the native land.

The project's architectural design and planning reinforces the contemporary Australian lifestyle. The large-scale complex is divided into six separate precincts that have unique names and visual expressions that are related to their merchandising. Clear wayfinding systems facilitate movement through the indoor and outdoor areas of the precincts.

The project is located between Melbourne and the Dandenong Ranges, a beautiful mountainous region that inspired a rich architectural vocabulary of local forms. The natural environment is echoed in the timber and lodge buildings, the palette of materials and patterns that recall the regional vineyards, and the broad verandas and lawns of the town square. Glazed façades, colorful décor, and bright lights enhance the energy of the urban marketplace.

3

4

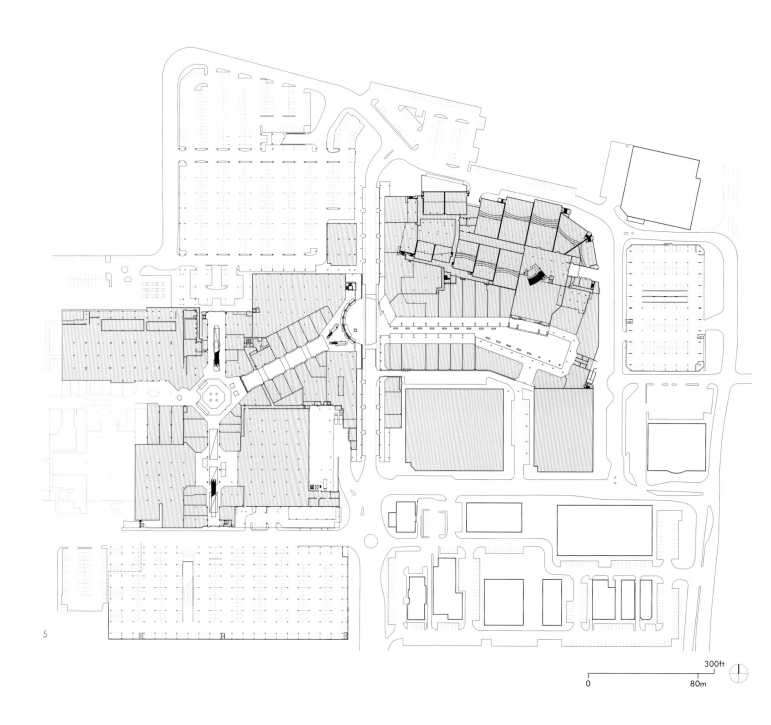

5   Site plan
6   Civic center
7   Retail gallery
8   View to street
9   Building detail

6

7

8

9

Design 2001

Boeing Realty Corporation

260 acres

PacifiCenter
Long Beach, California

1 Aerial plan
2 Office tower
3 Business park
4 Green space

The master plan for PacifiCenter converts a former Boeing plant located next to the Long Beach Airport and Interstate 405 into a state-of-the-art lifestyle community with an emphasis on business and technology. The 260-acre campus encompasses 5 million square feet of office space, two hotels, and a residential precinct, as well as 150,000 square feet of shops, restaurants, and services. Open spaces for passive and active recreation are dispersed throughout.

Lush, tree-lined streets and public gardens create a framework for the new neighborhood and create nodes of activity. Retail shops and restaurants define the rich and lively pedestrian environment and provide numerous opportunities for residents, workers and visitors to be outdoors. Major public amenities are clustered around a large open space known as "The Beach", which provides a focal point for the business and residential communities. The Beach combines the formal character of a European city square with the casual ambiance of the Southern California locale.

The project master plan incorporates sustainable principles that lessen its environmental impact, including systems to conserve and produce energy. High-capacity fiber optics and technological networks facilitate the needs of business.

2

3

4

5

6

7

5   Café on "The Beach"
6   Residential quarters
7   Residential courtyards

PacifiCenter   145

8 Public promenade
9 Paseo
10 Promenade
11 "The Beach"

1 Aerial view looking north
2 Aerial view looking south
3 Perspective from Metro Rail, looking south
4 View of mid-block office

Design 2005

OST Group

110,000-square-meter multi-use development, including 60,000 square meters of office space,
and 50,000 square meters of retail

Steel, glass

Yassenevo
Moscow, Russia

On the MCAT, the 83-mile transportation ring that encircles Moscow, stand multiple housing blocks built of precast concrete slabs in the post-WWII Soviet style. At Yassenevo, the dreary anonymity of the dense residential site is being transformed into a vibrant live, work, and play environment. The design brief calls for the addition of 60,000 square meters of office space and 50,000 square meters of retail/entertainment—all linked to parking, as well as bus and subway lines.

Situated between parallel housing blocks, the plan provides pedestrian access on all sides with the service areas cached in an interior passage. The office lobbies face onto the surrounding residential streets where their simple, modern, two-story glass entryways welcome passersby and workers. Atop the five- to eight-story buildings, glazed double-story spaces create a lantern effect that mirrors the entrance design.

The retail center, located at the back of the office towers, is reached via the internal pedestrian spine. Access is easy, sheltered, and offers visitors multiple opportunities for shopping and leisure.

Terracing down the hillside site, the dense urban composition uses a clean modern architecture to offset the brutalism of the housing. Materials include glass and metal panels with stone bases to protect against the wear and tear of the harsh Russian winter.

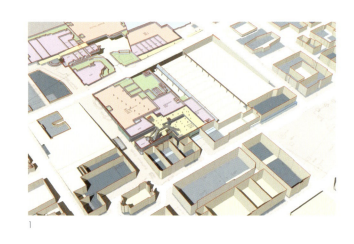

Design 2004
Buchanan Partnership
400,111 square feet

BUCHANAN GALLERIES
GLASGOW, SCOTLAND

Located at the nexus of the primary retail axes in the city of Glasgow, Scotland, Buchanan Galleries has long been a popular shopping destination. However, the owners and the City Council recognized that the shopping center had unrealized potential. The master planning team expanded the view of the project to include the broad context of the city's public realm as a means to enhance the retail offering and to improve the existing project as it relates to the Victorian and Georgian architecture that defines the urban fabric of Glasgow.

Evaluating the relationships among the transportation system, the nearby university, George Square, and other key places in the surrounding area, the design team identified multiple zones of influence. Through the invention of a diverse range of civic experiences within the project realm and the re-engagement of the project with the neighboring streets and public spaces, master planners created an urban design framework that allows the project to be of *the city*, not merely in the city.

Central to the redevelopment is a reorientation of the arrival experience that will bring customers to the new City Room adjacent to the historic Dundas Hose building and the Queen Street Train Station. This image-making civic space will serve as a landmark, a meeting point, and an entry portal to the expanded collection of galleries, each with their own identity and allure.

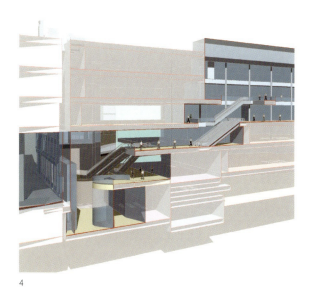

4

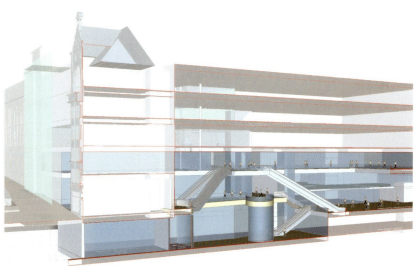

5

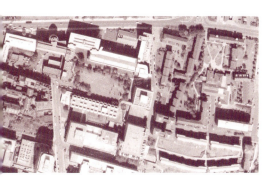

6

1 Transit as urban gateway — new arrival portal
2 Civic space linkage
3 Victorian/Georgian urban fabric
4 New Southern Gallery connection to multi-modal transit
5 Connectivity with transportation infrastructure
6 New Buchanan Galleries entry landmark

1 Residential/retail perspective
2 Residential entry perspective

Design 1994

PT Mulia Intipelangi (Mulia Group)

56-story, 1.2-million-square-foot office tower; five 38-story, 1800-unit condominium towers

Capitol Center
Master Planning and Conceptual Design
Jakarta, Indonesia

A mixed-use complex of six buildings raised atop a retail podium, Capitol Center is located in the Golden Triangle, one of Jakarta's most exclusive neighborhoods. The center includes a 60-story tower with prime office space; five luxury high-rise apartment buildings, each containing 1683 apartments and top-floor penthouses; retail facilities; and 5500 parking spaces.

The three-story retail atrium and parking facility provide structural support for the residential towers that are organized around an outdoor plaza above these low-rise buildings. Dispersed around the base of the residential buildings are private gardens with lush plantings, pools, lagoons, an orchid house, shaded paths, and facilities for active recreation. The residential towers have a staggered arrangement that maximizes unobstructed views. Four octagonal-shaped towers surround a slightly taller, square-shaped tower that completes the composition.

The office tower, which is clad in glass with granite spandrels and columns, is placed at a discreet distance from the residential buildings. Two façades of the tower curve gently, giving its rectangular shaft a distinct shape. A private entrance leads to three elevator banks that service the speculative offices spaces that are designed to American standards. Open floor plans allow panoramic perspectives of Jakarta.

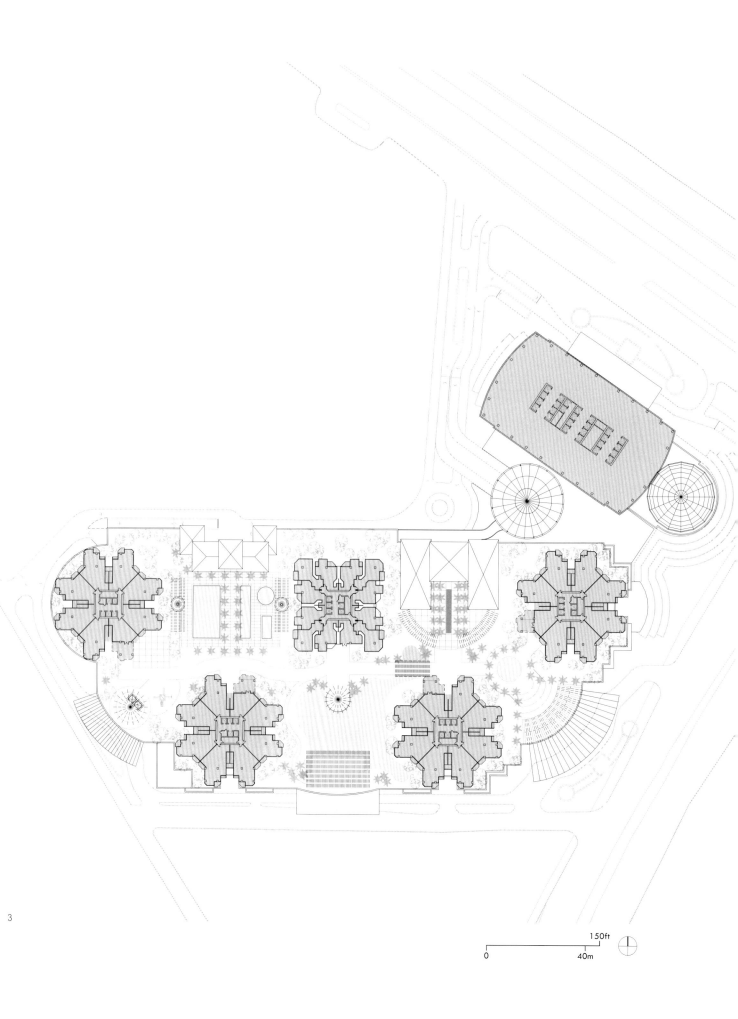

3　Site plan
4　Aerial view

Capitol Center　155

1 Perspective drawing
2 Daytime perspective
3 Plaza
4 Residential tower floor plan

Design 2001/Completion 2005

Robinsons Land Corporation

Two 35-story residential towers, one 40-story residential tower; 2000 condominium units

694,483 square feet GLA retail

Reinforced concrete structure, glass, aluminum curtainwall, natural stone, ceramic tile

Adriatico Towers
Manila, The Philippines

Plaza Adriatico is comprised of three residential towers and a new retail galleria that adjoin the existing Robinsons Ermita, a popular, mixed-use complex in historic Manila. The high-rise towers contain 2000 luxury condominium units overlooking the oceanfront that are anchored to the urban by retail and dining spaces in a three-story base.

The towers frame a broad public promenade at ground level. Lined by a collection of restaurants and cafés, the promenade creates a lively pedestrian precinct during the day and at night. The entrance to the retail base is distinguished by a multi-level glazed structure that draws visitors from the outdoor promenade to the venues inside.

Featuring sleek surfaces of glass and steel, combined with richly textured stone, Adriatico Towers matches the city's sophistication and style. Projecting metal cornices at the tops of the high-rise buildings create new landmarks for the Ermita district and the region at large. Integrated with lush tropical landscaping, the contemporary buildings add a distinction that transforms an older section of Manila into a vibrant residential neighborhood near the city's waterfront.

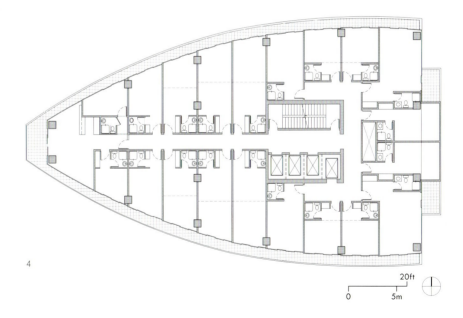

4

1 Office tower perspective
2 North perspective
3 East perspective
4 Site plan

1

2

3

Design 1994

PT Mulia Intipelangi (Mulia Group)

Two 68-story office towers; eight 36-story condominium towers;
3-level, 350,000 gross-square-meter retail center

Five Pillars
Jakarta, Indonesia

Located along a primary corridor between downtown Jakarta and the airport, Five Pillars creates a new center for business, residence, and regional shopping. The complex contains two 68-story office towers, eight 36-story condominium towers, a 350,000-square-meter retail center, and parking. The individual components are integrated into a balanced composition that establishes a sophisticated model for future development.

The office towers are the tallest buildings and the most visible. Glass curtain walls with stainless steel detailing and cantilevered, elliptical crowns reinforce strong rectilinear forms. Commercial facilities at the base of the towers connect the office buildings to the adjacent condominiums.

Clad in precast concrete, the residential buildings convey permanence and solidity, in contrast to the office towers' glazed façades. The residential buildings are placed on two parts of the site. Three octagonal buildings and two square towers are located across from the office towers atop a regional shopping center that contains retail stores, restaurants, and public services. Three additional residential buildings are located above a parking deck at the far end of the site. A continuous garden level that includes lush landscaping and a variety of recreational amenities connects the two residential areas.

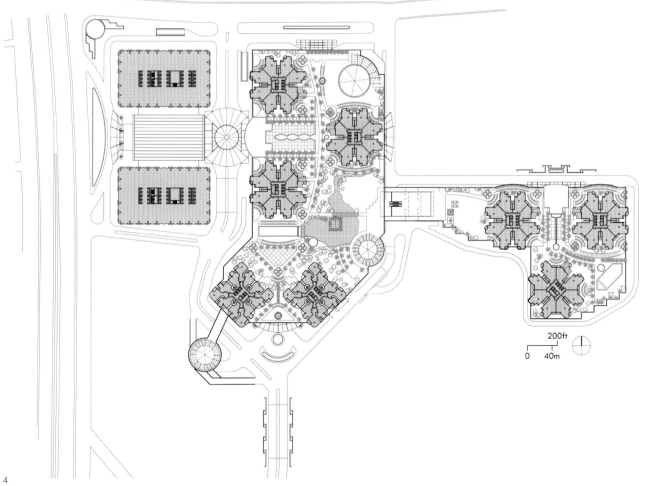

1 Food hall at night
2 View looking west along North Mainstreet
3 Building façade

Design 2002/Completion 2004

Forest City Development

1,300,000 square feet, 165 acres, 12 city blocks

Cement plaster, eifs, glass fiber reinforced concrete, limestone, sandstone, marble, granite, low-e glazing, masonry, ceramic tiles, wood, glass, metal panels, site-cast colored concrete, steel

Victoria Gardens
Rancho Cucamonga, California

Victoria Gardens establishes a traditional downtown for the growing Los Angeles suburb of Rancho Cucamonga. The 1.3-million-square-foot project is organized in an orthogonal grid that creates 12 open-air blocks on 147 acres that are carefully integrated with an adjacent residential community. The complex provides essential retail, residential, and office facilities that are commonly found in contemporary lifestyle centers. It also includes a complement of new civic uses that serve the diverse community.

The low-scale buildings define the city blocks and create a comfortable pedestrian environment. Office spaces are located above two-story retail shops that line the urban streets. Local architectural models, extending from the turn of the 19th century to the present, inspired the design of the buildings. This stylistic variety gives the buildings a sense of democratic individuality and the appearance of having been built over time. Civic functions are organized around a central town square and include a large children's performing arts theater, a conference center, and a public library.

The Gardens are located on a gently sloping site. Variations in the landscape emphasize the authentic and distinctive spaces that flavor the urban setting. Courtyards, paseos, pocket parks, and plazas accommodate both cars and pedestrians.

2

3

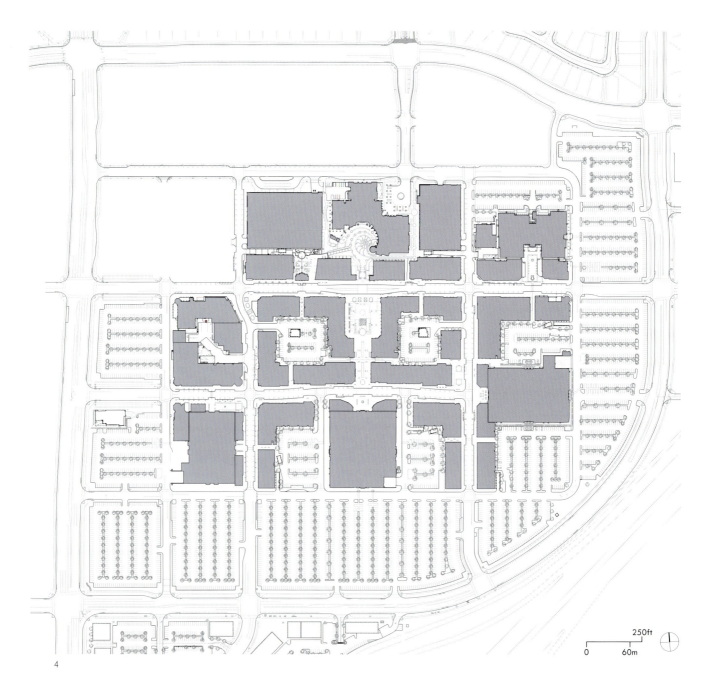

4

5

6

7

4   Site plan
5   Building façade
6   Looking east along South Mainstreet
7   Retail intersection
Following pages:
    Food hall interior

Victoria Gardens   163

City Rooms as Civic Space

Today Altoon + Porter Architects is working in urban centers around the globe on projects whose magnitude creates new meaning in the public realm. We endeavor to understand, interpret, and protect the legacy of the cities where we work. This effort is at the heart of our practice where the interconnected concepts of *Precedent — Evolution—Intuition*, first articulated by founding partner Ronald Altoon, guide our processes and establish our priorities in the design of civic space.

We embrace the opportunity and the obligation inherent in projects that repair the urban fabric. One of the greatest design challenges of our contemporary world is the vast swathe of public space that is simply residual, the unfortunate remnants of political or property skirmishes among defensive stakeholders. The results form an uninspiring domain that denies local communities deserved civic gathering spaces.

As urban designers, we mine for veins of design gold by exploring the rich strata of cultural, historical, political, environmental, and physical conditions of the urban context. We search to discover design values that will shape civic spaces of the city in the most positive fashion. We have learned to research, analyze, sketch, and communicate in ways that help us understand and define the nature of cities and the needs of citizens.

Working from a point of view that recognizes the value of diversity, we craft collections of spaces that in turn generate civic space. This is the foundation for projects that engage with the rhythm of a community. Our perspective enables us to create places that are capable of accommodating growth and adapting to unforeseen change. Over time our designs evolve in ways that we cannot initially imagine, in ways that make our projects good citizens.

Our vision encompasses not only buildings, although they are important civic assets, but also public spaces that we call City Rooms. True civic spaces create dialogue among the components—the architecture of the buildings, the open places, squares or plazas, and connections between them. City Rooms sit at the center of the urban experience, providing a framework for a multitude of activities that define civic life—from the everyday to the celebratory.

Ever mindful of the concept of public domain, we ask what it will feel like to move through the spaces we create. Will the space serve the community at large or is there a threshold that reads as private property? We analyze the connections between landmarks, as the experience along the path is often as important as the destination.

Recalibrating our focus, we examine the viability of reusing existing, seemingly redundant, structures that provide the historical or cultural texture of the public realm.

Looking to the future, we design for potential reinvention by another generation with other requirements. From our intuitive and research-driven processes we conceive and craft projects that fully belong to their locale and culture.

William J. Sebring, AIA
Partner

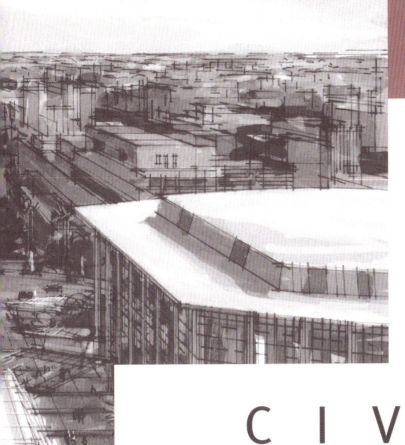

C I V I C I S M

The public spaces where people come together are as important as the buildings that house civic functions. Today's commons are as varied as their communities—from district-defining plazas to sheltered courtyards and inviting city rooms. Altoon + Porter Architects understands the importance of great gathering spaces as vital support for civic life. The work is marked by a sensitive use of building elements that engage their surroundings. Attention to scale and vista, and a sense of procession help to create spaces that invite civic participation.

1   Aerial perspective
2   Theater perspective
3   Perspective along Grand Avenue

Design 2000

The Music Center Performing Arts Center of Los Angeles

5 downtown city blocks

GRAND AVENUE URBAN DESIGN PLAN
LOS ANGELES, CALIFORNIA

For a few critical blocks, Grand Avenue is the heart of Los Angeles' cultural center, but it lacks the amenities to make it an inviting and accessible environment for patrons of the surrounding museums, theaters and concert halls. A series of four design workshops was held to organize, refine, test, and document an urban design plan for the Music Center of Los Angeles County. The stellar group included Frank Gehry, the architect of the Walt Disney Concert Hall; the architect of LA's Museum of Contemporary Art, Arata Isozaki; and Philadelphia landscape architect and urban planner Laurie Olin. Altoon + Porter, as executive architect, was the final member of the group.

The proposed plan rejuvenates the Music Center complex to create an environment that ensures maximum public accessibility and provides an oasis in the surrounding urban business and government environment. The concept improves the relationship of the Center to Grand Avenue and the under-utilized County Mall by realigning Grand Avenue, providing a wide sidewalk in front of the Center and bringing the plaza down to street level on Grand to make the entire plaza more accessible and welcoming. It also creates a greenway from the Center through the Mall to connect with public transit.

The redesign transforms the 35-year-old Music Center Plaza into an inviting urban public park spanning 11 acres, the length of the four-venue complex along Grand Avenue. The concept connects the existing three theaters at the Performing Arts Center, which includes the Dorothy Chandler Pavilion, the Ahmanson Theatre and the Mark Taper Forum, with the Walt Disney Concert Hall complex.

3

Grand Avenue Urban Design Plan   171

4

5

6

4&5   Study models
  6   Grand plaza/open-air theater
  7   Central park axis

7

Grand Avenue Urban Design Plan   173

8 Site plan
9 Grand plaza
10 Winter garden from Hope Street

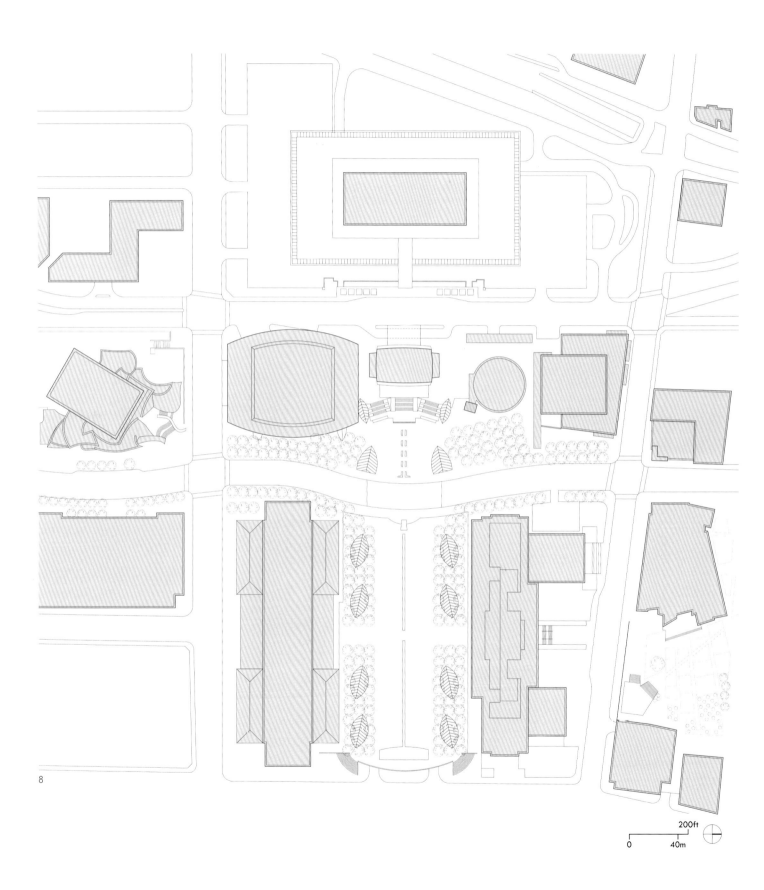

Grand Avenue Urban Design Plan

1

2

Design 1997/Completion 2005

Mass Transit Railway Corporation

1,500,000-square-foot retail and podium

Reinforced concrete structure, steel, glass, granite, terrazzo, stainless steel

KOWLOON STATION DEVELOPMENT
HONG KONG, CHINA

Because Hong Kong's new airport on Lanau Island is a major destination for thousands of passengers, it has become a major multi-modal transportation hub. At nearby Kowloon Station, the first and largest stop on the new rail line connecting Hong Kong, the design of a 12-million-square-foot mixed-use project featuring housing, hotels, office towers and retail takes advantage of the location to create a civic destination. Here travelers can check in for their flights at the convenient counter in the retail podium as local residents arrive to work, shop or play.

Set within the labyrinthine infrastructure of the transit system, the project delineates a distinct identity for each of the complex's uses while its open design connects the development to the surrounding neighborhood of busy Kowloon and creates a public space for civic use that is hard to find in the dense urban precincts of Hong Kong. The station's modernist aesthetic is softened by sleek, curvilinear forms and incorporates contextual elements from Hong Kong's world-famous harborfront. An abundance of natural light and color enlivens the interior spaces.

3

4

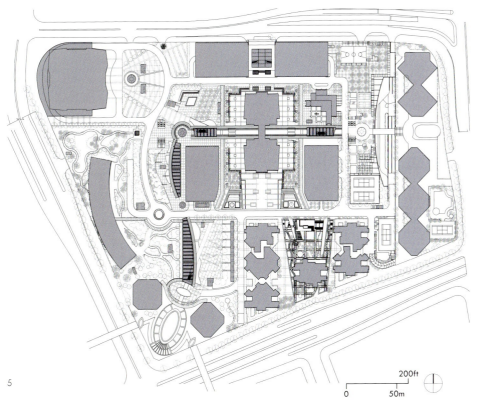

5

1 Aerial perspective
2 Podium level
3 Transit station entry
4 Central lobby
5 Site plan

Kowloon Station Development 177

1   Gallery stairs
2   Reception atrium
3   Park perspective

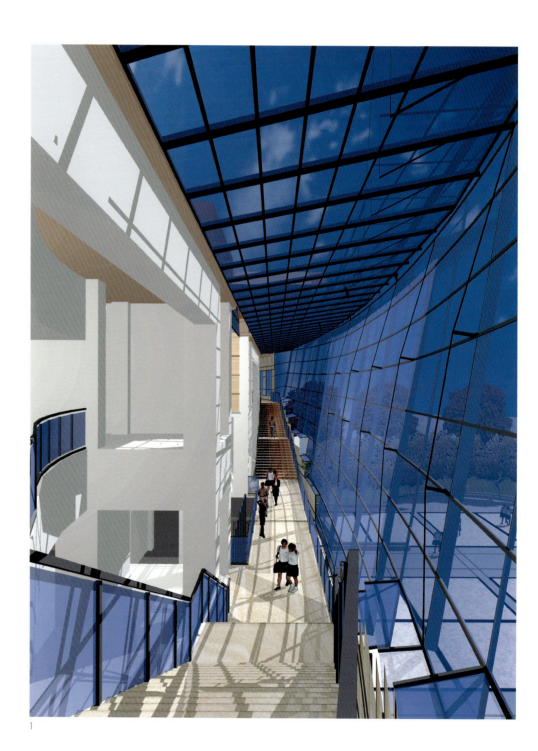

1

Design 1999

Crocker Art Museum

79,000 square feet

CROCKER ART MUSEUM
SACRAMENTO, CALIFORNIA

The Crocker Art Museum in Sacramento, California has continued to build on the legacy of 19th-century California art patrons, collectors, and founders, EB and Margaret E Crocker. Since the museum was established in 1885, the collections have grown well beyond both the original Victorian gallery and mansion and the late 20th-century addition.

The winning design proposal for an invited competition expands the canvas for the museum's vision to encompass an adjacent park, the edge of a commuter railway line, and public land enclosing a full city block. In addition to providing the museum room to appropriately house and organize the collections, the master plan creates an entire community arts campus. The new museum addition sited at the western edge of the campus presents a formal urban façade to the street while the park face of the building features a gracious, glazed façade that allows views across the park to the iconic State Capitol building.

The interior is organized as a series of served and servant spaces that facilitate the separation of the large viewing galleries away from the support spaces, security, and buildings systems that are critical to the function of the museum.

On axis with the main entrance, a multi-level gallery space in the new building looks out through the glass façade to the sculpture garden in the park.

4

4 Side elevation
5 Glass façade/park elevation
6 Street entrance elevation
7 Ground level plan
8 Upper level plan

5

6

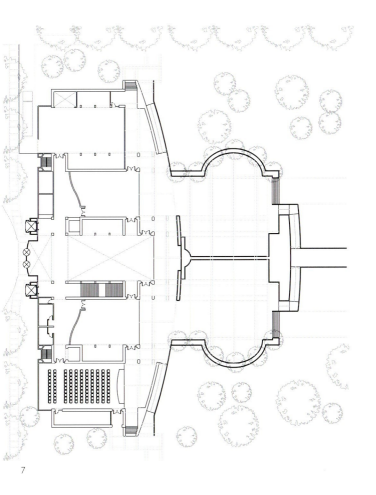

7

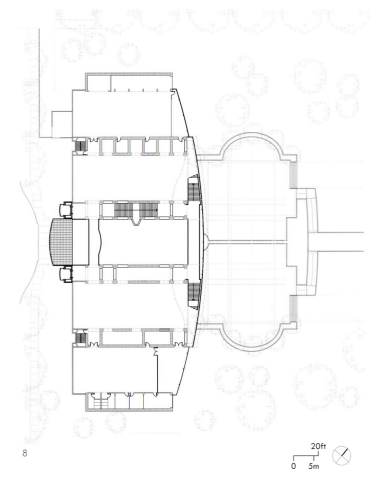

8

Crocker Art Museum 181

1 Gallery interior
2 Museum entrance
3 Site plan

Design 1986

Newport Harbor Art Museum and The Irvine Company

90,000 square feet

Newport Harbor Art Museum
Newport Beach, California

The Newport Harbor Art Museum, home to a highly respected collection of work by contemporary California artists, was part of a cultural campus that included a library. The museum planned to expand its facilities, despite its challenging hillside site, crisscrossed by utility lines and constraints such as height and setback requirements.

Plans called for the razing of the existing library building to provide space for the expansion of the museum and the addition of the community facility with a lecture hall and meeting space. The master plan then linked a new library building on the site to the museum through the insertion of a central gathering space.

An elongated gallery designed to house the permanent collection was located at the edge of the site on the hill where its linear form would act as an architectural billboard for the entire 90,000-square-foot cultural complex.

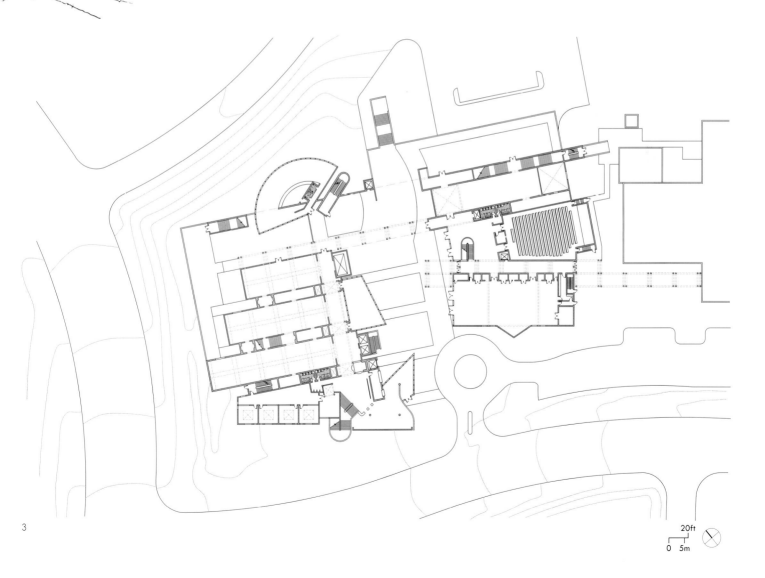

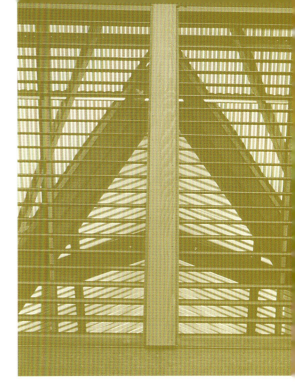

CULTURE

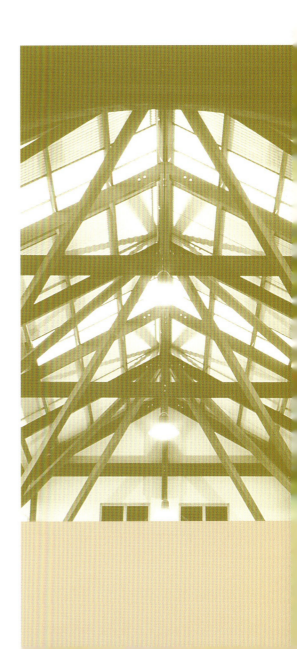

Societies, tribes, ethnic groups, and religions can be defined by their shared culture. The charge for Altoon + Porter Architects is to create environments that illuminate and nurture the vital aspects of those cultures, whether in the fine arts or in the quotidian rituals that bring people together. The effort begins in understanding cultural distinctions and ends in celebrating them with appropriate architecture.

1 Entry perspective
2 Site plan
3&4 Residential floor plans

Design 1994/Completion 1997

PT Mulia Intipelangi (Mulia Group)

Eight 36-story residential towers; 2900 condominium units

Taman Anggrek Condominiums
Jakarta, Indonesia

Southeast Asia's largest mixed-use residential and retail complex, Taman Anggrek is a sophisticated living and shopping destination that is distinctly Indonesian in character. The complex contains a total of 2900 luxury condominium units in eight 36-story residential towers and 1.5 million square feet of retail space. The multi-level retail center serves as the base for the towers and defines the urban edge of this "city within a city."

Named after the orchid gardens that once flourished on the site, the residential towers have flower-like floor plans. A traditional Indonesian fabric known as tapis inspired the rhythmic patterns that decorate the exterior façades of the towers. The flower theme is extended into the interior of the retail center that features a variety of waterfalls and indigenous plants.

A porte-cochere above the entrance to the retail center creates a grand sense of arrival. The center's large volume is divided into distinct, themed districts, and shops are organized around large public atriums. In addition to 700 stores, the center includes a 1200-seat food court and a multitude of entertainment destinations, including automobile showrooms, an ice-skating rink, games, a cineplex, and a disco.

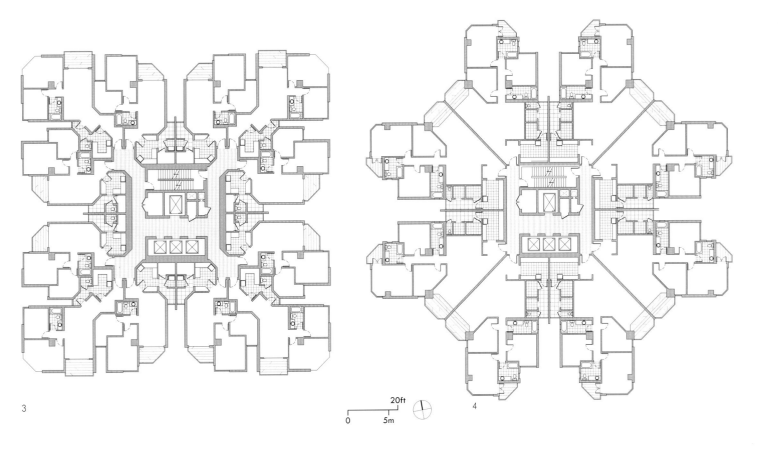

1 Iconic tower
2 Greenway to entry
3 Conservatory
4 Glass canopy
5 Main plaza

Design 1998/Completion 2001

AMP Henderson Global Investors

6,000,000 square feet

Natural stone, steel and glass canopies, painted cement, masonry, wood, and cement plaster

Botany Town Centre
Auckland, New Zealand

Botany Town Centre is a collection of diverse cultural destinations that form the downtown core of an emerging satellite community near Auckland. The mixed-use center combines office, retail, entertainment, and dining facilities that are integrated with Auckland's natural environment and adjoining residential communities. Regional and local buses serve the center.

The townscape is organized as a series of individual districts, ranging from the Fashion District to the Garden Walk, connected by pedestrian streets and passages. The distinct architectural identities of each district are unified around a central square. Parks, gardens, and waterways are filled with lush landscaping including flowering trees and fruit trees, and a conservatory depicts the Koury tree, one of the rainforest's most sacred specimens. Culturally significant but endangered flax plants are housed in an on-site arboretum.

Principles of sustainability determined the orientation of buildings, stormwater management, measures to reduce light production and water use, and systems to optimize energy performance. The wet but mild climate allowed for open and partially protected structures, in addition to fully enclosed buildings, in order to eliminate the cooling load.

6 Canopies
7 First level plan
8 Tower detail
9 Second level plan
10 Taxi station
11 Canopy detail
12 Entry gateway

6

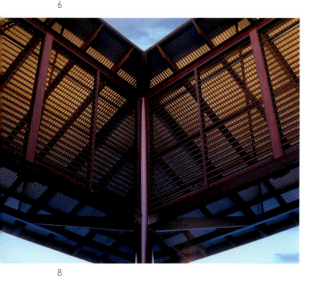

8

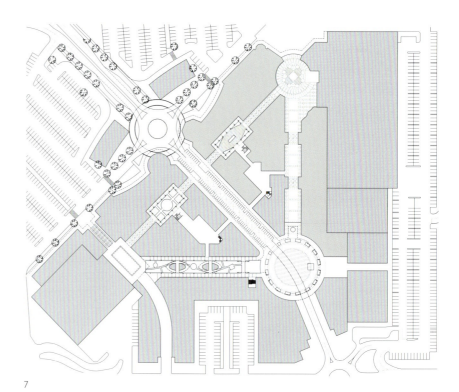

7

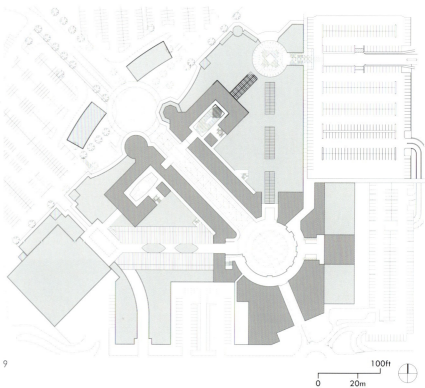

9

10

11

12

Botany Town Centre 191

13

14

15

13 Trellis ceiling detail
14 Bus stop
15 View though tower
16 Canopy detail
17 View to The Conservatory

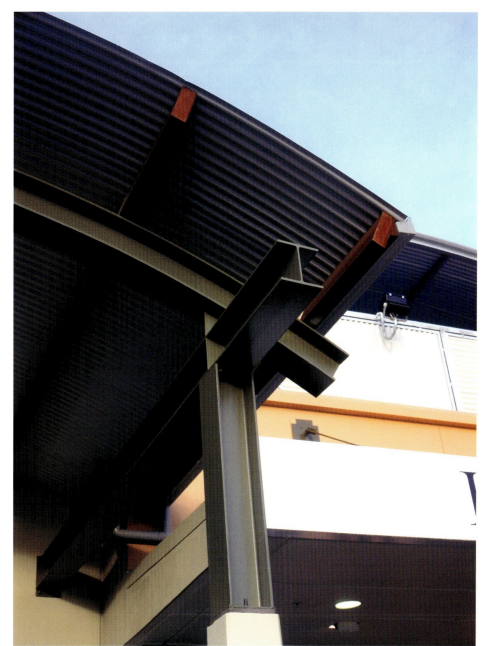

16

17

1 Town square entry
2 Site plan

Design 2003/Completion 2008

Corio Nederland Retail B.V. (retail center); ING Real Estate Development (housing)

90,000-square-meter retail center, 93 housing units

Masonry, stone, architectural concrete, stainless steel, frameless glass systems

Nieuw Hoog Catharijne
Utrecht, The Netherlands

Located in Utrecht's financial center, Nieuw Hoog Catharijne is a mixed-use residential/retail project that serves to connect the new train station and the convention center to the historic medieval square. New developments revitalizing the city include the return of a central roadway to use as a canal that runs directly underneath the project. The design celebrates the confluence of commerce, culture, and the canal with the introduction of a "City Room"—a large-scale glass box that spans the waterway.

The City Room serves as a civic gathering space that is always open to the public, offering views of the town and the renewed canal. At the same time, the design of the project provides a central linkage point among the latest additions to the urban mix, the old town and the older commercial district. The project is destined to become the heart of the community as it redirects the rhythms of urban activity.

The architecture reintroduces a Dutch sense of scale and restraint with a carefully delineated façade on the town square. Residents of the 100 units of housing atop the retail component will have ready access to the public space and amenities of the project.

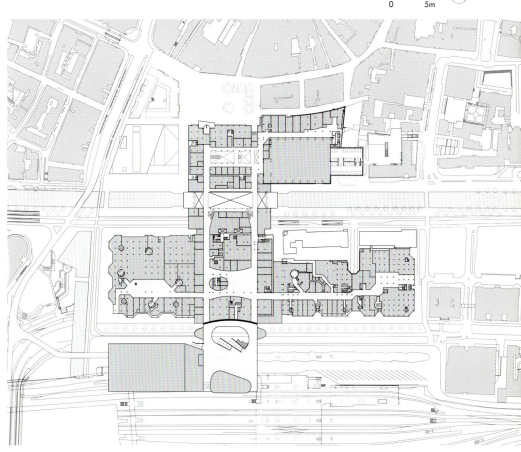

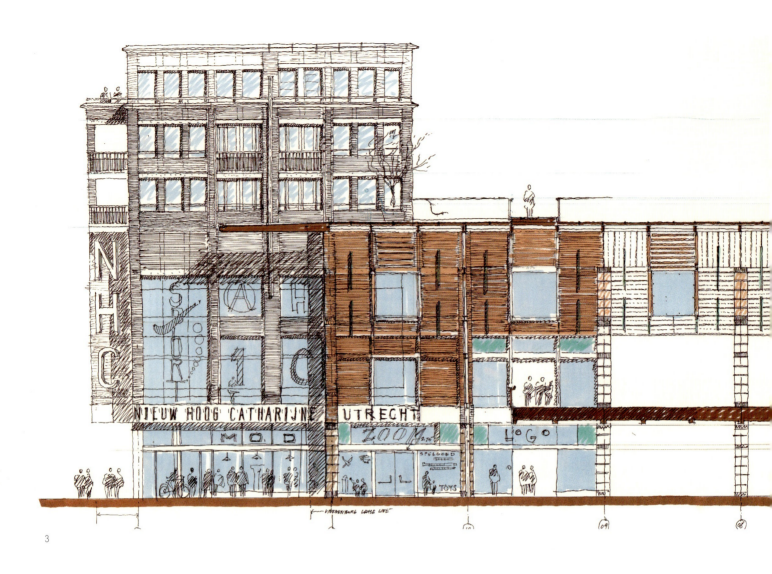

3 & 4   Sketch elevations
5   Canal view toward city room
Following pages
    Bird's-eye view perspective

5

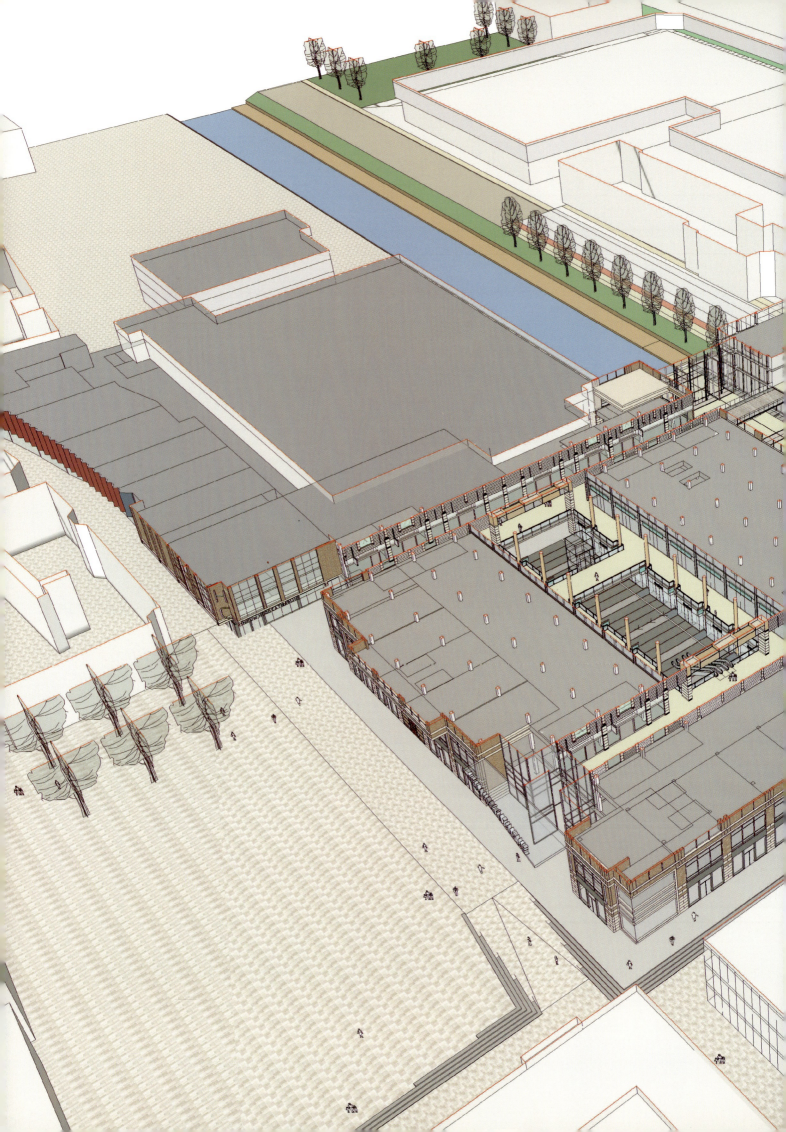

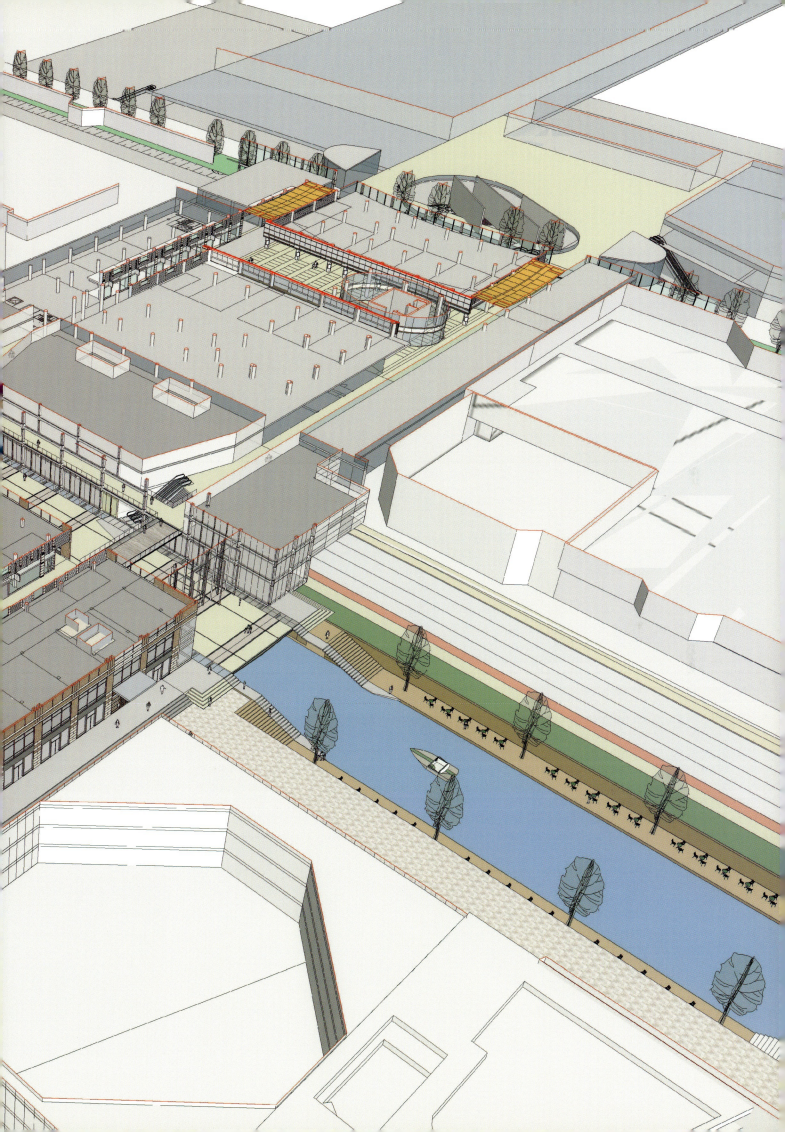

7

8

9

10

7 Historic canal restored
8 City room
9 Promenade park
10 City room over canal

1

2

3

4

Design 2003/Completion 2010

E.R.E. – European Retail Enterprise; Groupe B.E.G.

80,000 square meters

Metal canopy, steel tree columns, clerestory glazing, natural stone, limestone, terra cotta modular tile system, Gabion steel cage filled with river rock

Les Portes de Gascogne
Toulouse, France

Located on the outskirts of Toulouse in the southwest of France, Les Portes de Gascogne draws on the area's rich architectural traditions to create a new model for a shopping center. The Gascogne region is famed for its beautiful Bastides, early planned communities built around central civic spaces where people from the entire region gather for markets. The design of the new center celebrates the heritage of this concept with an inventive approach to modern retail.

The center features a collection of nine separate experiences that serve different shopping interests with distinctive character. Each of the multiple precincts—two fashion districts, specialty shops, a hypermarket–convenience district with off-price goods, a children's square, a lifestyle center, restaurants, leisure venues, and civic space—are linked through "portes" that create separate, memorable identities. Located near the central entrance is the high-volume, airy civic space that is crafted of exterior materials recalling the earth tone masonry of the region. A high-tech ceiling references the technological talents of local manufacturer Airbus.

Outside the complex, a market square reminiscent of the Bastides hosts local markets and links to a colonnaded pedestrian street where office space sits above the retail shops. Near the man-made lake, which is used to clean gray water from the complex for reuse, restaurants line the shore. Parking fields are cut into the landscape in the same way that traditional crops are cut into the surrounding fields.

1   Aerial perspective
2&5   Square and arcade
3   Along Les Arcade
4   Entry
6   Fashion passage

5

6

1 Central atrium
2 Women's Kingdom level
3 Main shopping level

Design 1997/Completion 2001

Kingdom Holding Co.

400,000-square-foot, 3-level retail center

Natural stone, stainless steel, glass, marble polished steel, bronze and stainless steel, perforated metal, frosted glass, wood paneling

AL MAMLAKA AT KINGDOM CENTRE
RIYADH, KINGDOM OF SAUDI ARABIA

At Al Mamlaka in the Kingdom Centre, Saudi Arabia's tallest building complex, a respect for Islamic culture shaped the design of the three-story retail center. While the first level is designed to appeal to young people and the leisure market, and the second level caters to fashion and home furnishings, the third level is reserved for women only.

Here in Saudi Arabia, home to the holy shrine of Mecca, the design puts the abbayeh—the veil worn by women—on the building to create a private bazaar within a bazaar for women shoppers. An exclusive, intimate environment with its own spa, business center and dining setting is conducive to an unrestricted shopping experience.

The entire retail complex is organized around a large central atrium where natural light streams through clerestory windows. Ceiling screens of perforated metal and sandblasted glass suspended from trusses transform and subdue the hostile desert sun and create super-scaled patterned surfaces befitting the grand hall. Three-story kiosks unify the design vertically while long bridges connect the floors horizontally, integrating the retail podium into the larger development as they provide access to adjacent offices, banks, the conference center, and hotel.

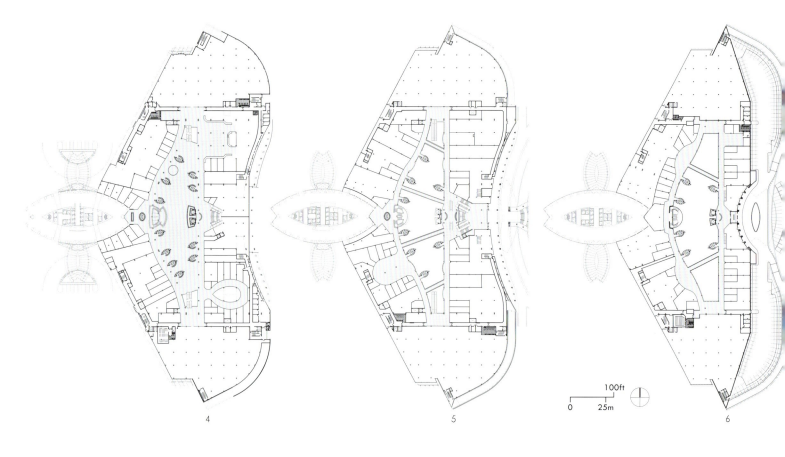

4 Level 1 floor plan
5 Level 2 floor plan
6 Level 3 floor plan
7 Porte-cochere for retail
8 Storefront
9 Food court
10 Three-level kiosk

8

9

10

Defining Legacy

Cam·pus NOUN: *pl.* cam·pus·es
   The grounds of a school, college, university, or hospital.

Com·mu·ni·ty NOUN: *pl.* com·mu·ni·ties
   A group of people living in the same locality and under the same government.
   A group of people having common interests or forming a distinct segment of society.
   Society as a whole; the public.

Sus·tain TRANSITIVE VERB: sus·tained, sus·tain·ing, sus·tains
   To keep in existence; maintain.
   To support the spirits, vitality, or resolution of; encourage.

Leg·a·cy NOUN: *pl.* leg·a·cies
   Something handed down from an ancestor or a predecessor or from the past.

Altoon + Porter is actively helping to sustain the built legacy of our region—the places, buildings, and public spaces that are true community treasures. While our work on these projects has not been our principal focus, it has significant influence on our practice. Our work on projects for commercial, retail, and mixed use clients is richer for our experience with public clients and, conversely, our work for the private sector affects our approach to public work. In fact, we see our perceived outsider status as an asset when working with government agencies, academic institutions, and cultural organizations because we are more willing to learn and to listen. Further, we are never afraid to question many long-accepted practices and procedures of these highly traditional organizations.

Consequently, we are seen as results-oriented versus process-oriented. In reality, we have a results-driven process rather a bureaucratic one and that allows us to better serve these institutions. A client once remarked that we seemed to understand their mission and willingly put our own mission second to theirs. As a practice we understand that our mission is to help the client achieve theirs. We succeed when we align the mission of good design with the mission of stewardship for the client.

The opportunity to design academic, governmental, and cultural projects for public and private constituencies is both a privilege and a responsibility. The projects are not simply historic preservation nor new buildings on greenfield sites. They are complex facilities that require us to weave the current and cutting edge carefully into the existing and often historically significant. Each situation, each problem, each circumstance requires its own specific solution.

We work in a very gentle way where the knitting of new and old is subtle and transformative. In every one of these projects we are, at once, respectful of the existing artifact and definitively creating architecture that is of this time and place. The expanded segments, fresh uses or complete new buildings are colored and massed in sympathy to the existing historic context, yet they stand on their own. These designs are healing gestures that give new faces to battered façades, improve the function of fragmented plans and integrate peripheral spaces.

The effort requires patience. It is an incremental approach that cross-pollinates with our work on commercial and mixed-use projects and draws upon our experience on other continents and in other cultures. The work is part of the long tradition of building that preserves and adapts and constantly reinterprets the architectural legacy in order to connect it in vital new ways to the contemporary community.

James C. Auld, AIA
Partner

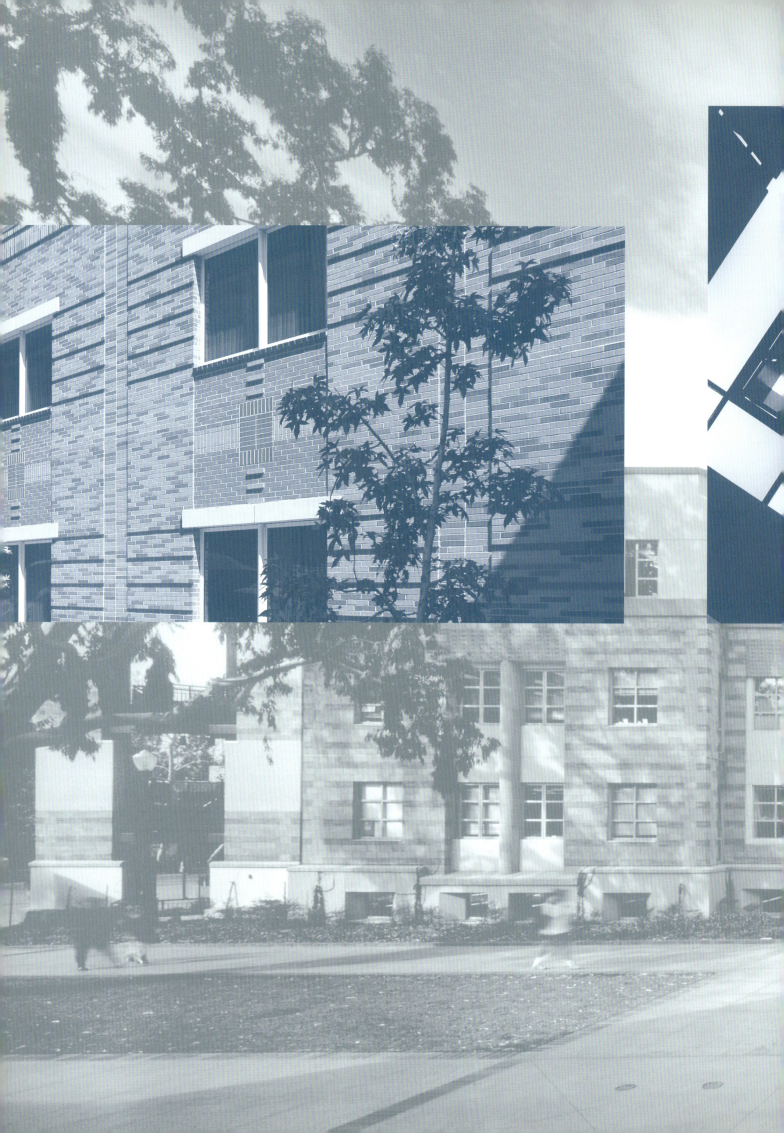

LEGACY

As the beneficiary of the historically rich context of the cities and campuses where it works, Altoon + Porter Architects seeks to extend these legacies with new architecture. The designers are sensitive to the enduring value of the architectural vocabularies that define environments, whether adapting a treasured building to current uses or adding new structures to the landscape. In designing for the current time and place, the firm is ever aware of its responsibility to the future.

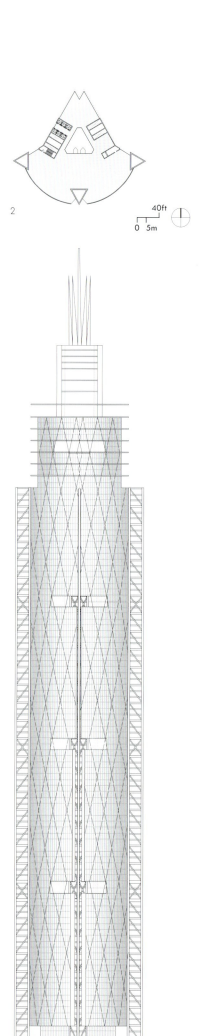

Design 1995

Dragon Bank

200,000-square-meter, 101-story office tower; 4 residential towers

DRAGON TOWER
JAKARTA, INDONESIA

Opposite   Office tower from southeast
2   South tower plan
3   South tower elevation
4   South elevation showing housing
5   Office tower from northeast

Located in Jakarta, Dragon Tower is a 101-story, mixed-use complex that fuses modern construction technologies and indigenous architectural elements. The five pillars that support the tower's massive superstructure refer to the five principles of the country's political philosophy or *Pancasila*. Four pillars buttress each of the four corners of the building. A taller pillar emerges from the top of the tower, creating a prominent landmark for Jakarta.

The tall, vertical façade rises in a series of terraces that were inspired by the temple structures of Borobodur, an ancient Javanese worship site. Diagonal bracing wraps the curving, glazed façade and protects the high-rise against the harsh Indonesian climate. The bracing creates an abstract design that refers to tapis, a local fabric that is commonly used for shelter.

The tower's clear glass skin is faceted to reflect light that filters into 24-story-high interior atriums that capture the vertical thrust of the tower. Public activities are concentrated on three transfer floors for express elevators to the tower's top. The transfer floors also act as sophisticated structural bridges that support the highest floors of the building, whereas the lower floors are braced horizontally at the tower's base.

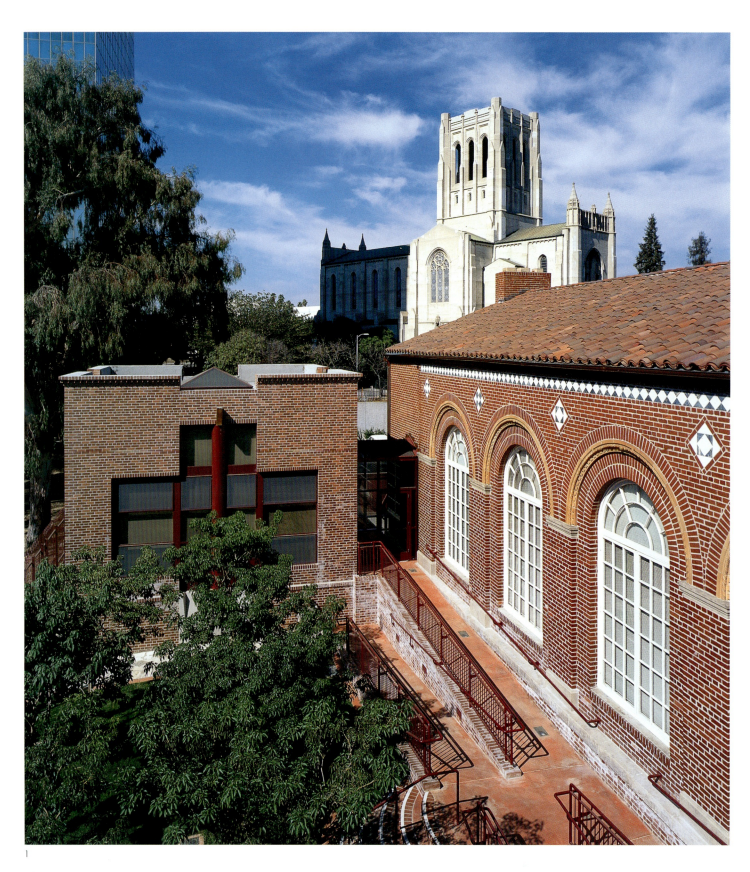

Design 1992/Completion 1998

The City of Los Angeles

5400-square-foot remodel; 1500-square-foot addition

Restoration of historic structure of brick and cement plaster; new steel structure with steel-framed windows

Felipe de Neve Branch Library
Los Angeles, California

The landmark 1929 Felipe de Neve Branch library in the Lafayette Park neighborhood of Los Angeles was returned to public use following a 5400-square-foot restoration, 1500-square-foot expansion and a seismic upgrade. Named in honor of the first governor of California and founder of Los Angeles, the building is listed on the National Register of Historic Places, an honor that subjected the project to additional scrutiny.

Working in close collaboration with officials from the City of Los Angeles and with local public artists, the architects designed an addition that echoes the formality and simplicity of the original plan. Two contemporary pavilions flank the original structure and create a link between the reading room and the terrace of a neighboring park. The pavilions, connected to the main building by glass arteries, define a semi-enclosed exterior space that is used as classrooms and reading areas.

Distinctive new rectangular windows contrast and complement the arched windows of the historic structure. The windows were strategically placed to accommodate library features including the bookshelves. Interior spaces are open with minimal partitions to allow for easy supervision from the reference desks.

1 Reading courtyard perspective
2 Park façade

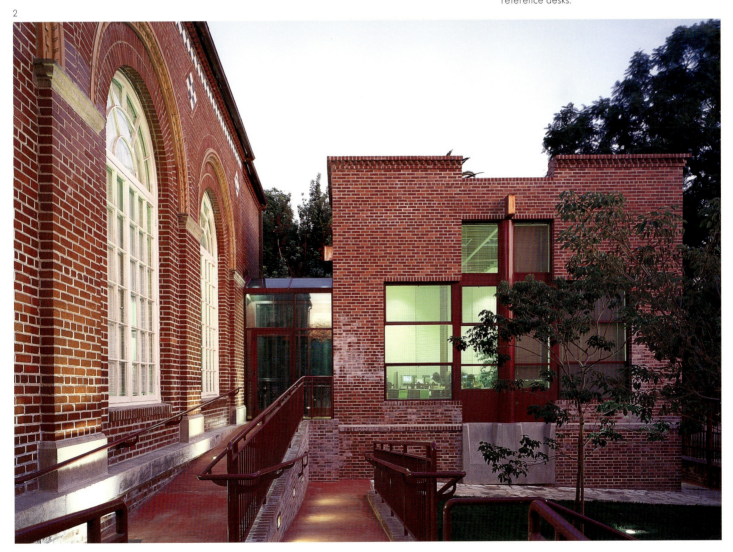

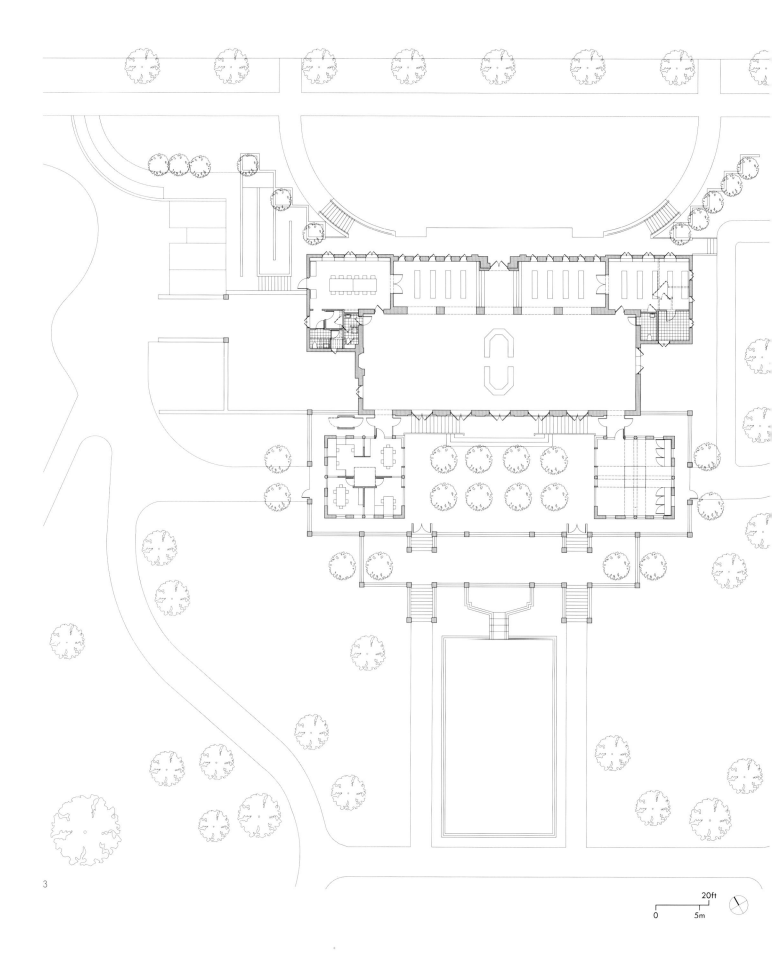

3 Site plan
4 Window detail
5 Children's reading room
6 Skylight over offices

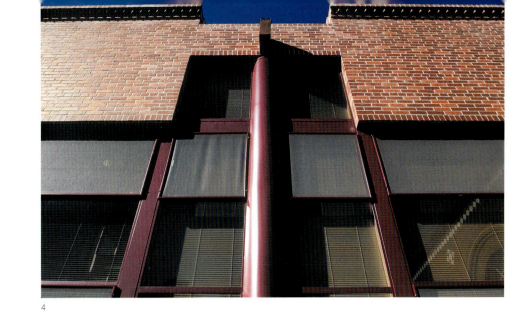

4

5

6

1

2

Design 1992

The Getty Conservation Trust

4000-square-foot classroom platform area

Steel, Teflon-coated fiberglass

Siqueiros Mural Shade Structure
Los Angeles, California

The Siqueiros Mural shade structure honors the beauty and history of *America Tropical*, a mural that was completed by famed Mexican artist David Alfaro Siqueiros in 1932 on the site of the city's original Hispanic settlement. Long considered to be a controversial work, the beloved cultural artifact remains a sacred icon for the city's Latino community.

The shade structure combines an innovative design and state-of-the-art technology to give the mural the intense respect and visibility that it deserves. Sponsored by the Getty Conservation Institute, the shelter creates a public destination and a forum for educational events while protecting the work, which had fallen into a critical state of disrepair, from future environmental damage and exposure to the sun's ultraviolet rays. Seating and audio-visual equipment, including a projection screen, enhance educational opportunities.

The lightweight shelter creates a pedestal for the project that uplifts and enshrines the artwork. Above the mural, a layered canopy of translucent scrims forms an awning composed of curved, rotating elements that modulate exposure to the elements. A bridge that floats over the surrounding commercial district provides access to the mural. Dramatic views of the mural are framed by the delicate metal structure, and perimeter ramps allow wheelchair access within 10 feet. When the mural is illuminated at night, the canopy glows softly.

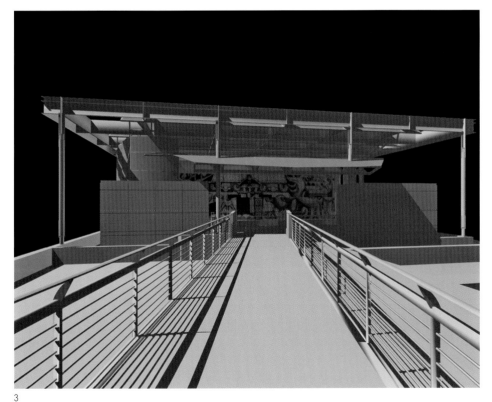

3

1 Aerial view
2 Plan
3 Viewing platform

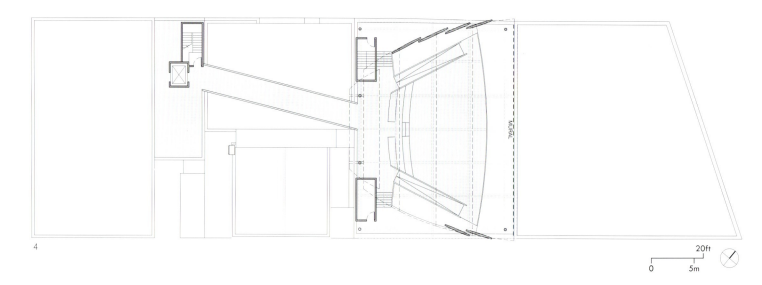

4 Platform plan
5 Historic mural
6 Roof plan

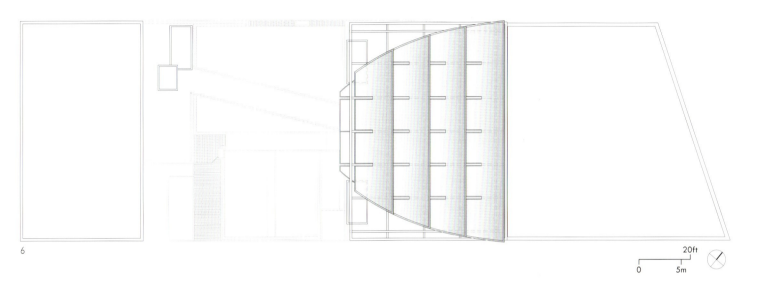

6

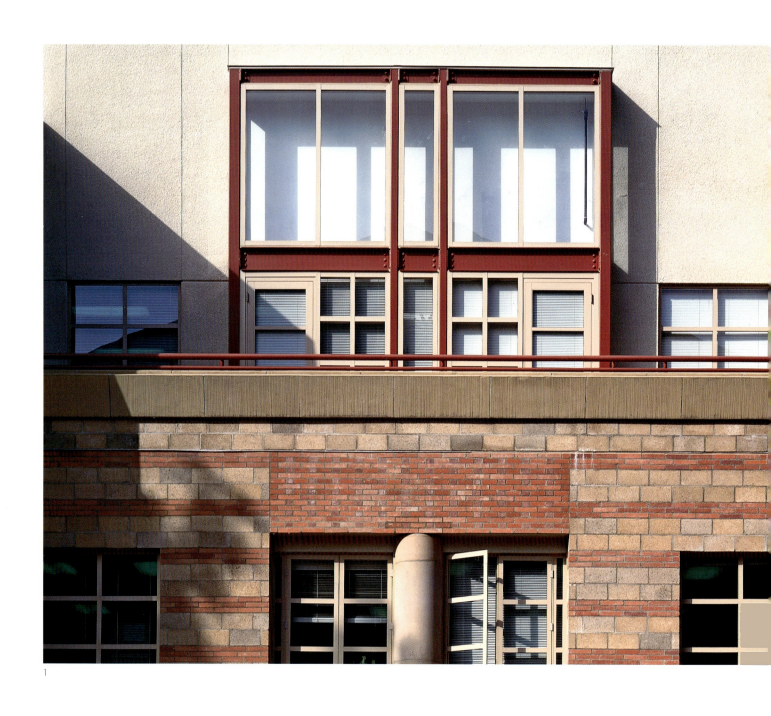

Design 1992/Completion 1993

University of California, Los Angeles Programs Design and Construction

40,000 square feet

Full exterior brick and concrete block, steel, glass

Arthur Ashe Student Health and Wellness Center, UCLA
Los Angeles, California

The expansion of the John Wooden Center provided the university with the opportunity to restore the harmony and formal order intended by the original master plan at a key crossroads on the campus. Years of growth and differing design visions resulted in a variety of architectural styles from three eras. The early campus buildings were designed in the Northern Italian Romanesque style—monumental in scale, yet intimate in detail. Post-World War II science buildings were designed in an over-scaled, international style. Coldly sculptural, the more recent buildings are wedged uncomfortably between the buildings of the other eras.

The original Wooden Center building, a late addition, sat facing an elegant original landmark, separated by a primary pedestrian artery. By surrounding the existing stucco box with a thin "sliver" building, the new design gives the structure the first of three designed façades that reflect the Romanesque scale and aesthetic. A mixture of brick and buff-colored concrete block, plaster, and terra cotta tiles complements the Romanesque revival neighbor. The design is in harmony with the historic campus core, while the brickwork and plaster banding create a distinct new image for the building.

Using simple elements to connect the building to its historic context, the architecture created a working framework for future additions. A flexible structure designed and constructed in twelve months, it accommodates administrative, student health, temporary student union, and credit union functions. The tower aptly anchors and defines Bruin Plaza, the crossroads of campus activity.

1 Façade detail
2 New masonry

2

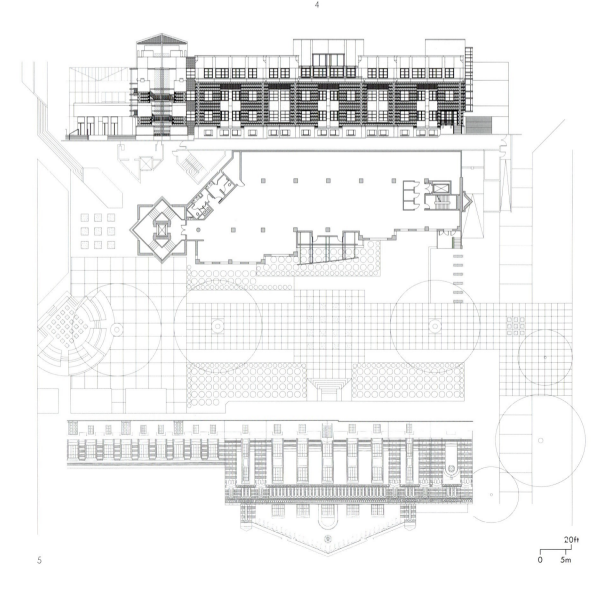

3 Historic masonry
4 East façade
5 Plans and elevations
6 Tower detail
7 East façade

Arthur Ashe Student Health and Wellness Center, UCLA

1 Glazed entry pavilion
2 View to parking under soccer field

1

Design 1994/Completion 2001

University of California, Los Angeles Programs Design and Construction

32,000 square feet

Full exterior brick and concrete block, steel, glass

JOHN WOODEN RECREATION CENTER NORTH AND WEST EXPANSIONS, UCLA
LOS ANGELES, CALIFORNIA

By expanding the John Wooden Center to the north, the athletic facility gained 32,000 square feet of additional space for interim and permanent activities related to a number of athletic and other University programs. The subsequent western addition to the John Wooden Recreation Center connects to the north addition to provide 40,000 square feet of additional recreational and administrative space. A new glazed entry pavilion identifies the northwest corner of the building where the west and north additions connect.

The north and west façades of the existing structure were expanded on two levels. The corridors and vertical transportation systems of the John Wooden Center were extended directly into the additions to create a seamless connection with the existing building. Together, the two additions provide necessary upgrades, including locker rooms for the existing Recreation Center, state-of-the-art dance, aerobic, and fitness rooms with double floating hardwood floors, and classrooms for military science instruction. Offices and multifunction spaces for the Recreation Department and the ROTC programs of the Armed Services were also incorporated.

Clad in two types of brick banding, terra cotta tile, and plaster, the additions complement the historic buildings of the campus, as well as the new Arthur Ashe Student Health and Wellness Center, which is located on the east side of the Recreation Center. The choice of materials enabled the University to complete a cost-effective, long-term solution for its needs. The additions were designed in conjunction with the new varsity soccer and lacrosse field, and a below-grade parking structure under the field that accommodates 1250 cars.

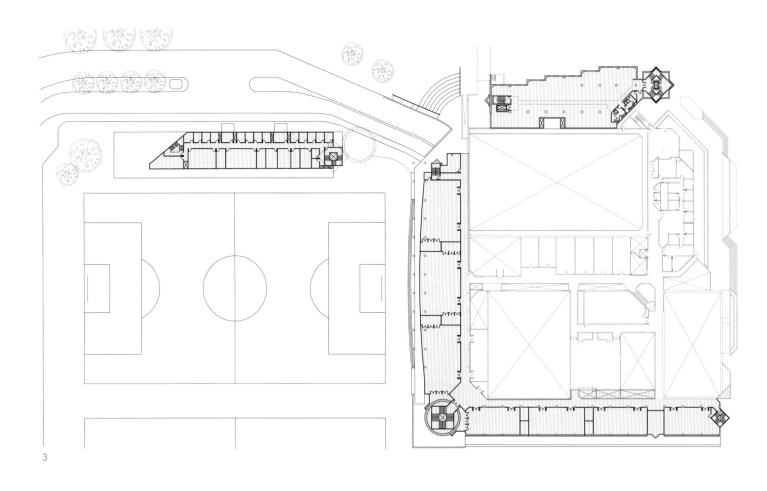

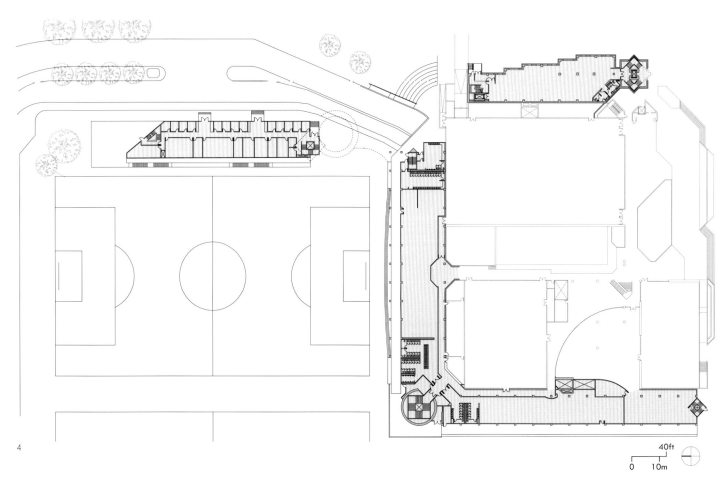

3 Second level plan
4 Ground level plan
5 Stadium view

1

2

Design 2000/Completion 2003

University of Southern California

14,500 square feet

Full brick, precast concrete, mission tile, glass

USC School of Social Work Center
Los Angeles, California

On a small, constrained site on the edge of the University of Southern California, the expansion of the School of Social Work Center reaffirms the architectural legacy of the campus. As an outreach program, the School of Social Work required both a welcoming face for the outside community and an increase in space that encourages interaction among students. The design takes advantage of an infill opportunity on the highly developed urban campus to transform land previously used for on-grade parking into an inviting academic environment.

The project expands the Montgomery Ross Fisher School of Social Work with 14,500 square feet of classrooms, offices, and a student lounge. Along the northern edge of the University Campus, the design creates a new façade for the school. At the same time, the new wing joins the existing buildings to form a south-facing courtyard that is shielded from the noise and traffic of nearby Jefferson Boulevard.

The design carefully blends old with new to reinforce the architectural vocabulary of the campus. Stone bases, window sills, parapet edges, as well as major façade elements, are rendered in cast stone and form a visual bridge that encompasses the cast concrete elements found in the 1970's building and the limestone building elements from buildings at the core of the historic campus.

3

1 North elevation
2 Courtyard view
3 South elevation

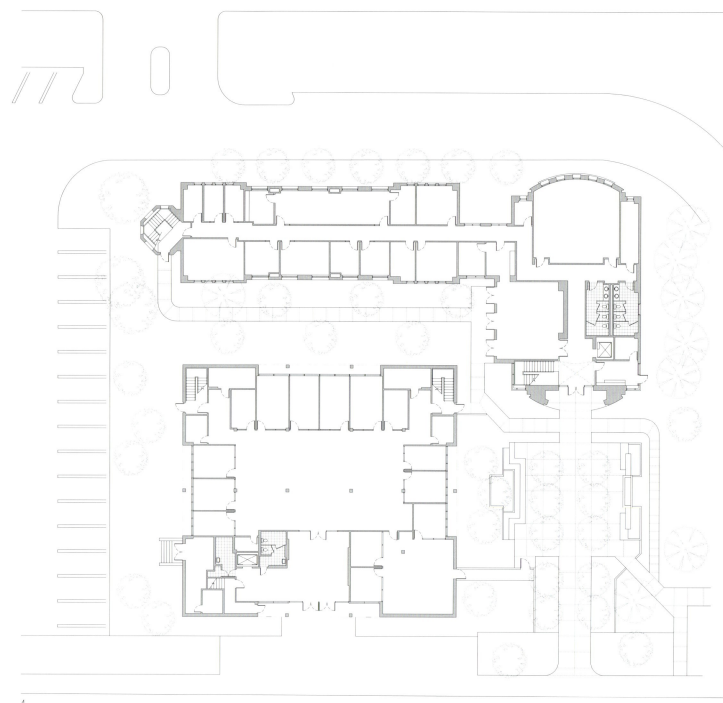

4

5

6

4 Site plan
5 North façade
6 Building detail
7 Second level plan
8 Window and masonry detail
9 Walkway along south façade

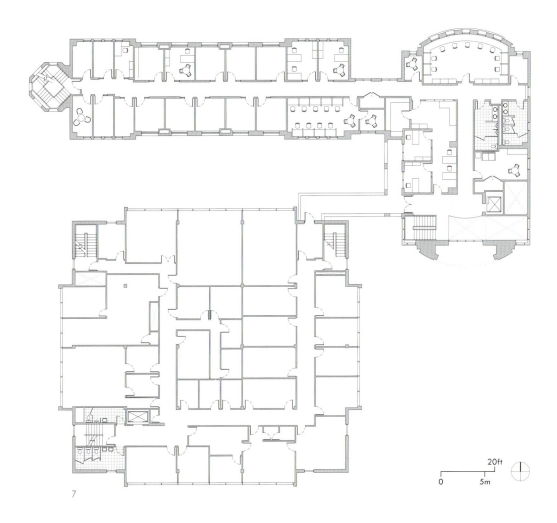

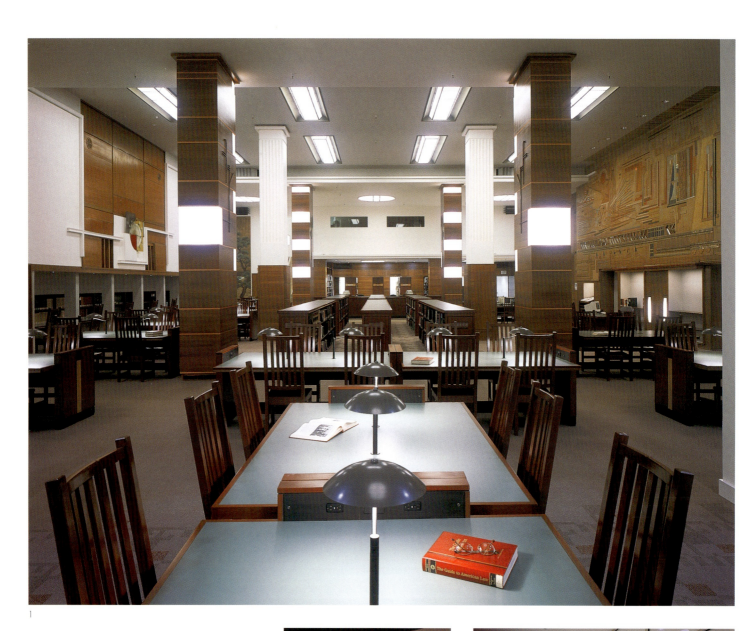

1

2

3

1 Main reference room
2 Stacks
3 Computer classroom
4 Historic tower
5 Study area
6 Reference room and stacks

Design 1992/Completion 1997

Southwestern University School of Law

87,000 square feet to house 365,000 books

Historically restored terra cotta wall tiles, cooper roof, marble floors, wood paneling, original art, fittings and fixtures; new glass, custom carpets, furniture and fixtures

SOUTHWESTERN UNIVERSITY SCHOOL OF LAW LIBRARY
LOS ANGELES, CALIFORNIA

The conversion of the former 1929 Bullocks Wilshire department store building into a state-of-the-art library for the Southwestern University School of Law posed a dual challenge: to preserve the famous architectural details of the so-called "Cathedral of Commerce," and to incorporate new furniture and building systems into an ideal location for contemporary study and research. Upgrades included the integration of cutting-edge technology, computer labs, study rooms, networked seating, and open book stacks for 365,000 books.

Two project designers collaborated on the project to provide individual expertise in historic preservation issues and the sophisticated technical systems required for the library. The restoration process involved extensive historic building and "archaeological" research in order to recapture and enhance the building's finest features, including the original decoration of former displays, delicate woodwork, patterned floors, and intricate murals.

Library functions were seamlessly inserted amid the beauty of the Art Deco interiors. The layout respected the subdivision of the building into small rooms that once served as retail boutiques. Custom-designed furniture, including bookcases with warm tones and patterns that recall clothing display racks, reflects the craftsmanship and character of the original store. All mechanical systems were upgraded and barrier-free design standards were maintained throughout.

4

5

6

7

9

8

7 Historic elevator detail
8 Custom furnishings and fixtures
9 Stairwell
Opposite Restored murals

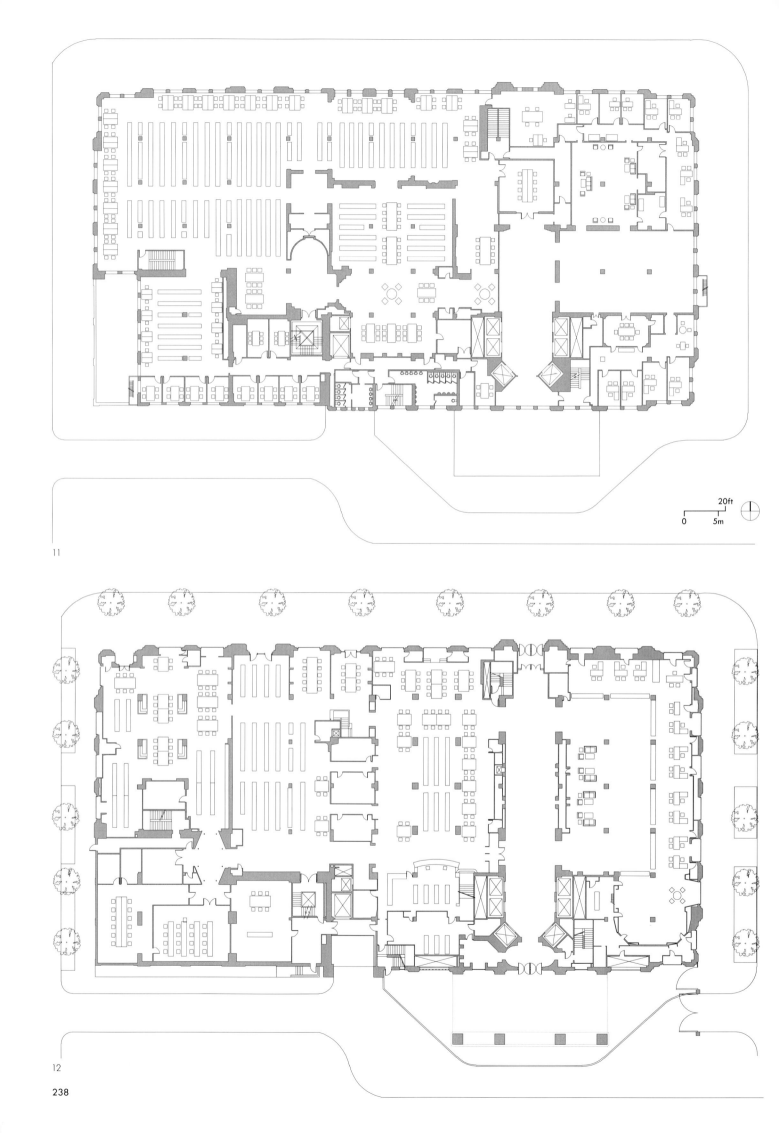

13 View from street
14 Carrels and stacks
15 Study area

11 Second floor plan
12 First floor plan
13 View from street
14 Carrels and stacks
15 Study area

Fractals of Architecture

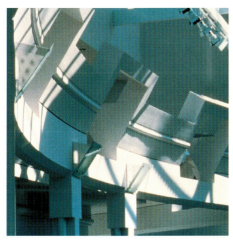

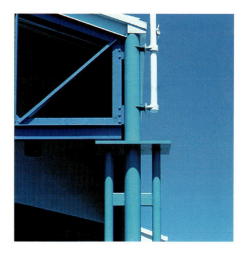

Fractals of Architecture

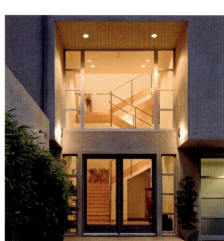

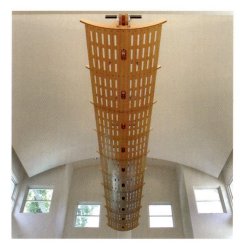

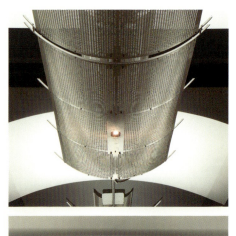
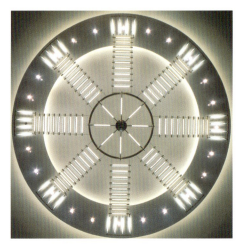

Fractals of Architecture

Chronology of Projects

1986
Newport Harbor Art Museum
Newport Beach, California
Newport Harbor Art Museum and The Irvine Company

Redmond Town Center
Redmond, Washington
Winmar Company

UCLA Ackerman Union Renovation
Los Angeles, California
Regents of the University of California

1987
3275 Wilshire Boulevard Offices
Los Angeles, California
Altoon + Porter Architects

5657 Wilshire Boulevard (Pereira Building)
Los Angeles, California
Metro Arts Partners

9570 Wilshire Boulevard (Wilshire-Camden)
Beverly Hills, California
Gilbert Financial Corporation

The Brockman Building
Los Angeles, California
USA Pacific Atlas, Inc.

The Crossroads
Irvine, California
The Irvine Company and Diversified Shopping Centers

Engine Company Number 28
Los Angeles, California
Management Compensation Group

Fort Worth Town Center
Fort Worth, Texas
Texas Centers Associates

The Grand Avenue
Los Angeles, California
Private developer

The GrandWay
El Segundo, California
Sutter Hill and M&S Development

Three Las Vegas Center Master Plan
Las Vegas, California
Dean A. Beck & Associates

1988
Fannie Mae Corporate Headquarters
4000 Wisconsin Avenue Building
Washington, DC
The Holladay Corporation and The Donohoe Companies

Altius Mixed-Use Master Plan
Palm Desert, California
Carver Companies

Gresham Station
Gresham, Oregon
Winmar Company/Trimet

Villa Marina
Marina del Rey, California
GBW Properties

Wilshire/Harvard Office Building
Santa Monica, California
Latigo Corporation

Wilshire/St. Andrews Office Building Renovation
Los Angeles, California
Winston Millet

1989
Artists Building
Marina del Rey, California
GBW Properties, Inc.

Earthquake – MCA Universal Studios
Universal City, California
MCA Universal Studios

Lido Marina
Newport Beach, California
Aosta-Lido Interests

Marina Marketplace
Marina del Rey, California
GBW Properties Inc.

Master Plan for the Town of Spitak
Soviet Republic of Armenia
USSR Government

1990
Arden Fair
Sacramento, California
Homart Development Co.

Calabasas Promenade
Calabasas, California
Pazar Associates

Forest Park Mall
Chicago, Illinois
Bennett & Kahnweiler Companies

King Kong – Universal Studios Florida
Orlando, Florida
MCA Universal Studios – Florida

KTA Future Pavilion
Seoul, Korea
Supertek Productions

Lincolnwood Town Center
Lincolnwood, Chicago, Illinois
Melvin Simon & Associates and Hawthorne Realty Group

Manufacturing Facility
Leninakan (Gumri), Republic of Armenia
Armenian Assembly of America, Inc.

Market Square at Arden Fair
Sacramento, California
Morton and Marcy Friedman and Dennis Marks

Seven Bridges
Chicago, Illinois
Forest City/Harris Group

1991
5700 Wilshire Boulevard Offices
Los Angeles, California
Wilshire Courtyard

Carew Tower Historic Renovation and Adaptive Reuse
Cincinnati, Ohio
Emery Realty Co.

Century Plaza Towers Concourse
Los Angeles, California
Prudential Realty Group and JMB Realty Corporation

The Mall at Green Hills
Nashville, Tennessee
General Growth Center Companies, Inc.

Osceola Multi-Use Development
Orlando, Florida
Disney Development Companies

RKO Pictures, Inc.
Multiple Locations
RKO Pictures

Tower Place
Cincinnati, Ohio
Faison Associates & Noro Realty Advisors

1992
Manhattan Village
Manhattan Beach, California
TCW Realty Advisors

One Wilshire Building
Los Angeles, California
The Paramount Group

Siqueiros Mural Shade Structure
Los Angeles, California
The Getty Conservation Trust

Sherman Oaks Galleria Renovation
Sherman Oaks, California
Prudential Insurance Company of America and LaSalle Partners
General Growth Center Companies, Inc.

Spring Hills Mall
West Dundee, Illinois
TCW Realty Advisors and Homart Development Co.

Triangle Square
Costa Mesa, California
Triangle Square Joint Venture

1993
Broadway Plaza
Los Angeles, California
Cushman & Wakefield

Sherman Oaks Galleria Garden Offices
Sherman Oaks, California
Galleria Joint Venture, Prudential Insurance Company of America and LaSalle Partners, and General Growth Center Companies, Inc.

NFL – Youth Education Training Center
Compton, California
National Football League

North Hills
Raleigh, North Carolina
North Hills Inc.

Pacific Financial Plaza
Newport Beach, California
California State Teachers Retirement Systems

UCLA Arthur Ashe Student Health & Wellness Center
Los Angeles, California
University of California, Los Angeles Programs Design and Construction

1994
Capitol Center
Jakarta, Indonesia
PT Mulia Intipelangi (Mulia Group)

Five Pillars
Jakarta, Indonesia
PT Mulia Intipelangi (Mulia Group)

Ka'ahumanu Center
Maui, Hawaii
Maui, Land & Pineapple Company, Inc.

La Jolla Village Square
La Jolla, California
Gordon/Beck Ventures and Solus Property Company

Metropolis
Hawthorne, California
Mission Land Company

Pluit Hotel and Shopping Center
Jakarta, Indonesia
PT. Mulia Griya Indah

1995
Alderwood Mall
Lynwood, Seattle, Washington
The Edward J. DeBartolo Corporation

Bighorn Institute
Palm Desert, California
Bighorn Institute

Dragon Tower
Jakarta, Indonesia
Dragon Bank

MCA Universal Offices
Universal City, California
MCA Universal

UCLA Parking Structure 3
Los Angeles, California
University of California, Los Angeles Programs Design and Construction

1996
Echo Horizon School
Culver City, California
Echo Horizon Foundation

Kota BNI Train Station
Jakarta, Indonesia

Pico/San Vicente Joint Development
Los Angeles, California
Metropolitan Transportation Authority

1997
Al Maktoum Road
Dubai, United Arab Emirates
Al Ghurair Group

Beverly Premier
Southern California
Private developer

Denver West
Denver, Colorado
TrizecHahn Centers Management, Inc.

Fashion Valley Center
San Diego, California
ERE Yarmouth, Inc.

Los Arcos
Scottsdale, Arizona
Ellman Companies

Bur Juman Centre
Dubai, United Arab Emirates

Murrieta Hot Springs Master Plan
Murrieta Hot Springs, California
Donahue Schriber

Santa Margarita Town Center
Rancho Santa Margarita, California
The Koll Company and Santa Margarita Company

Shaikh Zayed Road
Dubai, United Arab Emirates
Al Ghurair Group

Southwestern University School of Law Library
Los Angeles, California
Southwestern University School of Law

Taman Anggrek Condominiums
Jakarta, Indonesia
PT Mulia Intipelangi (Mulia Group)

Van Nuys Municipal Courthouse Renovation
Van Nuys, California
County of Los Angeles Internal Services Department

1998

Felipe de Neve Branch Library
Los Angeles, California
The City of Los Angeles

The Gardens on El Paseo
Palm Desert, California
Madison Realty Partnership

Kaleidoscope
Mission Viejo, California
Samsung PDP Kaleidoscope, LLC

Oceangate Curve
Hawthorne, California
Mission Land Corporation

Valencia Retail Entertainment Center
Valencia, California
The Newhall Land & Farming Company

Warringah Mall
Brookvale, New South Wales, Australia
AMP Henderson Global Investors

1999

Crocker Art Museum
Sacramento, California
Crocker Art Museum

Downtown West Dearborn
West Dearborn, Michigan
D.J. Maltese Co.

The Shops at Mission Viejo
Mission Viejo, California
Simon Property Group

Mucha Centre
Prague, Czech Republic
European Property Development

Parly 2
Le Chesnay, France
Societe des Centres Commerciaux

Valencia Offices and Retail
Valencia, California
The Newhall Land & Farming Company

Warringah Mall – Phase II
Brookvale, New South Wales, Australia
AMP Henderson Global Investors

2000

444 South Flower Street Offices
Los Angeles, California
Altoon + Porter Architects LLP

2000 Residence
Los Angeles, California
Private owner

Amgen European Logistic Center Expansion
Breda, The Netherlands
Amgen

Flatiron Marketplace
Broomfield, Colorado
Koll Development Company

Go2Town
Taoyuan, Taipei, Taiwan
Tai-Tung Development Company
(a division of Taiwan Pulp & Paper Corporation)

Pavilions at Houston Center
Houston, Texas
Crescent Real Estate, Equities, Inc., and Entertainment Development Group

Grand Avenue Urban Design Plan
Los Angeles, California
The Music Center Performing Arts Center of Los Angeles

Redondo Beach Marina
Redondo Beach, California
Mar Ventures, Inc.

Vedanta Society Campus
Hollywood, California
Vedanta Society

The Waterfront
Marina del Rey, California
Vestar Development Company

2001

Al Mamlaka at Kingdom Centre
Riyadh, Kingdom of Saudi Arabia
Kingdom Holding Co.

Amgen Inc. Campus Plan
Thousand Oaks, California
Amgen, Inc.

Auchan Competition
Suburban site, Italy
Auchan Ipermercati Grouppo Rinascente, sponsored by L'Arca

Botany Town Centre
Auckland, New Zealand
AMP Henderson Global Investors

Centre Commercial de Massy
Massy, France
Altarea

Chodov Centrum
Prague, Czech Republic
Rodamco Ceska Republika

Hollywood & Highland
Hollywood, California
TrizecHahn Development Corp.

Inland Center
San Bernardino, California
Chase Investors and General Growth Center Companies

Kirkgate Quarter
Leeds, United Kingdom
Stannifer

Macy*s Prototype
Lakewood, California
Federated Department Stores, Inc.

Marina Square
Singapore
Marina Square Holdings

MultiCasa Development
Duisburg, Germany
TrizecHahn Europe

PacifiCenter
Long Beach, California
Boeing Realty Corporation

SetúCentre
Setúbal, Portugal
Filo S.A.

UCLA John Wooden Recreation Center North and West Expansion
Los Angeles, California
University of California, Los Angeles Programs Design and Construction

Zhung-Guan Village International School
Hai-Dian District, Beijing, China
Beijing Topeak Real Estate Development Company

2003

Fashion Show
Las Vegas, Nevada
The Rouse Company

Knox City Centre
Melbourne, Victoria, Australia
AMP Henderson Global Investors

USC School of Social Work
Los Angeles, California
University of Southern California

Valencia Town Center Expansion
Valencia, California
The Newhall Land & Farming Company

2004

Buchanan Galleries
Glasgow, United Kingdom
Buchanan Partnership

Victoria Gardens
Rancho Cucamonga, California
Forest City Development

2005

Sengkang Station
Singapore
Land Transportation Authority

Adriatico Towers
Manila, Philippines
Robinsons Land Corporation

Aurora Mall
Aurora, Colorado
Simon Property Group

Brea Mall Food Court
Brea, California
Simon Property Group

Buangkok Station
Singapore
Land Transportation Authority

Carrara Place Compound
Los Angeles, California
Porter Development

Kowloon Station Development
Hong Kong, China
Mass Transit Railway Corporation

The Shops at Tanforan
San Bruno, California
Wattson-Breevast

USC Law School Library
Los Angeles, California
University of Southern California

USC School of Fine Arts
Los Angeles, California
University of Southern California

2006

Antelope Valley Mall Renovation
Antelope Valley, California
Forest City Development

Brea Mall Lifestyle Center Master Plan
Brea, California
Simon Property Group

Central World Plaza
Bangkok, Thailand
Central Pattana Property Investment & Development

FaFa Mall
Guangzhou, China
Goldsun Group

Mozaica – Third Ring
Moscow, Russia
OST Group and Groupe B.E.G.

UCSB California NanoSystems Institute
Santa Barbara, California
University of California, Santa Barbara

Waikiki Beach Walk
Honolulu, Hawaii
WBW LLC

IN PROGRESS

Exotic Animal Training Management Facility, Moorpark College
Ventura, California
Ventura County Community College District

Fort Bonifacio Global City
Manila, Philippines
Ayala Land, Inc.

Good Zone
Moscow, Russia
Fenix Development

Les Portes de Gascogne
Toulouse, France
E.R.E. – European Retail Enterprise / Groupe B.E.G.

Nieuw Hoog Catharijne
Utrecht, The Netherlands
Corio Nederland Retail B.V. (retail center); ING Real Estate Development (housing)

Paramaz Avedisian Building – American University of Armenia
Yerevan, Armenia
American University of Armenia

The Shoppes at Chino Hills
Chino Hills, California
Opus West Corporation

Shoreline Gateway
Long Beach, California
AndersonPacific LLC

Windward Mall
Kaneohe, Hawaii
Kamehameha Schools and General Growth Properties, Inc.

Yassenevo
Moscow, Russia
OST Group

Yoho Town
China
Sun Hung Kai Properties Ltd

Design Awards

24th Annual Preservation Award
Los Angeles Conservancy
Southwestern University School Of Law Library
at Bullocks Wilshire
Los Angeles, California
2005

**Design Award for Innovative Design
and Construction of a New Project**
International Council of Shopping Centers
Botany Town Centre
Auckland, New Zealand
2003

**Design Award for Innovative Design
and Construction of a New Project**
International Council of Shopping Centers
Al Mamlaka
Riyadh, Saudi Arabia
2003

Auchan Competition
*Auchan Impermercalt Gruppo Rinascente
Architettura, Immagine ed Emozione concorso
internazionale di architecttura*
Prototype Suburban Site in Italy
2001

**Design Award for the Renovation
or Expansion of an Existing Project**
International Council of Shopping Centers
The Shops at Mission Viejo
Mission Viejo, California
2001

National Preservation Honor Award
The National Trust for Historic Preservation
Southwestern University School of Law Library
Los Angeles, California
2000

Honor – Renovation Design Award
*The American Institute of Architects,
Pasadena/Foothill Chapter*
Southwestern University School of Law Library
Los Angeles, California
2000

Honor – Unbuilt Design Award
*The American Institute of Architects,
Pasadena/Foothill Chapter*
Siqueiros Mural Sun Shade Structure
Los Angeles, California
2000

**Merit Award, Design for Sustainability –
Energy & Resource Efficient Solutions**
*The American Institute of Architects,
Pasadena/Foothill Chapter*
Ka'ahumanu Center
Kahului, Maui, Hawaii
2000

Merit – Commercial Design Award
*The American Institute of Architects,
Pasadena/Foothill Chapter*
Ka'ahumanu Center
Kahului, Maui, Hawaii
2000

**Design Award for Innovative Design
and Construction of a New Project**
International Council of Shopping Centers
The Gardens on El Paseo
Palm Desert, California
2000

**Design Award for the Renovation
or Expansion of an Existing Project**
International Council of Shopping Centers
Warringah Mall – Stage I
Sydney, Australia
2000

**Respectful Renovation Award #1
In Recognition of 1997 Restoration
and Adaptive Re-use**
*Windsor Square – Hancock Park Historical
Society*
Southwestern University School of Law Library
Los Angeles, California
1999

**Design Award for the Renovation
or Expansion of an Existing Project**
International Council of Shopping Centers
Fashion Valley Center
San Diego, California
1999

**Design Award for Innovative Design
and Construction of a New Project**
International Council of Shopping Centers
Santa Margarita Town Center
Rancho Santa Margarita, California
1999

Design Award for Museum
Crocker Art Museum
Sacramento, California
1998

Historic Preservation Award of Excellence
City of Los Angeles Cultural Heritage Commission
Southwestern University School of Law Library
Los Angeles, California
1997

**Rose Award, Renovation & Historic
Preservation Top Honors**
*The Downtown Breakfast Club, Los Angeles,
17th Annual Roses and Lemon Design Awards*
Southwestern University School of Law Library
Los Angeles, California
1997

**27th Annual Urban Beautification
Architectural Awards**
Remodeled Institutional Projects
Los Angeles Business Council
Southwestern University School of Law Library
Los Angeles, California
1997

Commendation for a New Addition to a Historic Public Building
City of Los Angeles Department of Cultural Affairs
Felipe de Neve Branch Public Library
Los Angeles, California
1996

Design Award for the Renovation or Expansion of an Existing Project
International Council of Shopping Centers
Ka'ahumanu Center
Kahului, Maui, Hawaii
1996

Design Award for the Renovation or Expansion of an Existing Project
International Council of Shopping Centers
Market Square at Arden Fair
Sacramento, California
1996

Commendation for Historic Preservation
City of Los Angeles Cultural Heritage Commission
Felipe de Neve Branch Public Library
Los Angeles, California
1995

Design Award for the Renovation or Expansion of an Existing Project
International Council of Shopping Centers
The Mall at Green Hills
Nashville, Tennessee
1995

Design Award for Innovative Design and Construction of a New Project
International Council of Shopping Centers
Triangle Square
Costa Mesa, California
1994

Design Award for Innovative Design and Construction of a New Project
International Council of Shopping Centers
Tower Place
Cincinnati, Ohio
1993

Historic Preservation Honors
City of Los Angeles Cultural Heritage Commission
Engine Company Number 28
Los Angeles, California
1992

Design Award for the Renovation or Expansion of an Existing Project
International Council of Shopping Centers
Arden Fair
Sacramento, California
1991

Certificate of Merit for Innovative Design/New Project
International Council of Shopping Centers
Lincolnwood Town Center
Chicago, Illinois
1991

Co-Winner, Renovated Enclosed Mall
Mall Monitor
Arden Fair
Sacramento, California
1991

Honorable Mention, New Enclosed Mall
Mall Monitor
Lincolnwood Town Center
Chicago, Illinois
1991

Award of Merit
Chicago Lighting Institute, Division of the Electrical Association
Lincolnwood Town Center
Chicago, Illinois
1991

Certificate of Honor
The Structural Engineers Association of Illinois
Lincolnwood Town Center
Chicago, Illinois
1990

9th Annual Rose and Lemons Design Awards, Rose Award, Renovation
Downtown Breakfast Club, Los Angeles
Engine Company Number 28 – Restaurant
Los Angeles, California
1989

19th Annual Beautification Award for Remodeled Commercial Low-Rise
Los Angeles Business Council
Engine Company Number 28
Los Angeles, California
1989

Centers of Excellence Award Honorable Mention
National Mall Monitor
The Crossroads
Irvine, California
1989

Honor Award
American Planning Association, Washington Chapter
Redmond Town Center
Redmond, Washington
1988

7th Annual Preservation Award
Los Angeles Conservancy
Engine Company Number 28
Los Angeles, California
1988

8th Annual Rose and Lemons Design Awards, Rose Award, Top Honor Renovation
Downtown Breakfast Club, Los Angeles
Engine Company Number 28
Los Angeles, California
1988

Consultants and Collaborators

Altoon + Porter wishes to thank Nancy Egan for her editorial contribution to this book.

444 South Flower Street Offices
Structural engineer: Robert Englekirk Consulting Structural Engineers, Inc.
MEP: Syska & Hennessy
Mechanical contractor: ACCO
Contractor: Swinerton & Walberg
Photography: Wayne Thom, Rowland Heights, California; Ronald A. Altoon, FAIA

2000 Residence
Photography: Wayne Thom

5700 Wilshire Boulevard Offices
Mechanical engineer: Tsuchiyama & Kaino
Electrical engineer: Fredrick Russell Brown & Associates
Lighting designer: Wheel Gersztoff Friedman Shankar Inc.
General contractor: Howard Rosenfeld, Inc.
Photography: Fred Licht, La Cañada, California; Erhard Pfeiffer, Los Angeles, California

Adriatico Towers
Client: Robinsons Land Corporation
Associate architect: W.V. Coscolluels & Associates Architects
Architectural illustration: Scott Lockard, Lockard Creative, Kentfield, California

Al Mamlaka at Kingdom Centre
Al Mamlaka, retail center architect: Altoon + Porter Architects LLP
Kingdom Centre architect/engineer: Consortium of Ellerbe Becket, Inc. and Omrania & Associates
Technical architect/engineer and construction supervisor: Omrania & Associates
Structural engineer: Ove Arup & Partners
Mechanical/electrical engineer: The Building Services Group Ltd.
Quality surveyor: Cotton Thompson & Cole
Safety code: Rolf Jensen & Associates, Inc.
Security: Schiff and Associates
Vertical transportation: Lerch Bates & Associates
General contractor: El Seif Engineering Contracting Establishment
Photography: Joe Poon, Riyadh, Kingdom of Saudi Arabia

Bighorn Institute
Structural engineer: David D.B. Johnson Structural Engineer
Mechanical engineer: Double O Engineering
Electrical engineer: Nikolakopulos & Associates
Civil engineer: ASL Consulting Engineers
Construction/specification: Ralph P. Mellman & Associates
Soil engineer: Earth Systems Consultants
Contractor: Lyle Parks Jr. General Contractor
Photography: Erhard Pfeiffer

Botany Town Centre
Associate architect: Hames Sharley International Ltd.
Project manager: Bovis McLachlan
Structural engineer: Buller George
Service engineer (M/E): Lincolne Scott
Civil engineer: Tonkin & Taylor Ltd.
Acoustic engineer: Kingett Mitchell & Associates Ltd.
Landscape architect: Natural Habitats
Graphic designer: Peter Haythornewaite Design
Public art artist (Kauri Tree): Elizabeth Thompson
Lighting designer: Light Works Ltd.
Traffic design: Traffic Design Group
Artist: Elizabeth Thompson
General contractor: Mainzeal Construction
Photography: Grant Sheehan Photography, Wellington, New Zealand; Michael Ng Photography, Auckland, New Zealand; Ronald A. Altoon, FAIA

Buangkok Station
Associate architect: 3HP, Singapore
Lighting consultant: Francis Krahe & Associates, Inc.
Photography: Albert Lim KS, Singapore

Carrara Place Complex
Photography: Wayne Thom; Erhard Pfeiffer

Central World Plaza
Local architect of record: A49
Local landscape architect: L49
Local interior architect: IA49
Local graphics: G49
Landscape architect: SWA Group
Environmental graphics: Redmond Schwartz Mark Design
Lighting designer: Kaplan Gehring McCarroll Architectural Lighting
Curtain wall consultant: DVV Associates
Façade engineer: Arup
Computer Visualization: A-3D, Bangkok, Thailand

Chodov Centrum
Associate architect: Atelier 8000, Prague, Czech Republic
Structural engineer: Kupros, Zizkov, Czech Republic
Building services engineer: Tebodin Czech Republic s.r.o., Karlin, Czech Republic
Landscape: Delta Vorm, Groep, Utrecht, Czech Republic
Geodetic survey: J+F, Prague, Czech Republic
Traffic: Denis Wilson Partnership, s.r.o., Prague, Czech Republic

Exotic Animal Training and Management Facility, Moorpark College
Structural engineer: John A. Martin & Associates, Inc.
Mechanical/plumbing: M-E Engineers, Inc.
Civil engineer: Penfield & Smith Engineers & Surveyors
Acoustical engineer: McKay Conant Brook, Inc.
Construction cost estimator: C.P. O'Halloran Associates, Inc.
Theater consultant: Auerbach • Pollock • Friedlander

Echo Horizon School
Structural engineer: Johnson & Nielsen Associates
Mechanical engineer: Double O Engineering
Electrical engineer: Nikolakopulos & Associates
Landscape architect: Melendrez & Associates
Civil engineer: Mollenhauer, Higashi & Moore, Inc.
Soils engineer: Geotechnical Professional, Inc.
Artist: Guy Dill, Venice, CA
Contractor: Del Amo Construction, Inc.
Photography: Erhard Pfeiffer

Fashion Show
Conceptual design: Richard Orne, AIA, Orne & Associates and Laurin B. Askew, Jr., FAIA, Monk LLC
Design manager for The Rouse Company: Richard Orne, AIA, Orne & Associates
Structural engineer: Ove Arup & Partners; ASI; SME Steel Contractors
Mechanical/plumbing: Tsuchiyama & Kaino
Electrical engineer: Patrick Byrne & Associates
Electrical: B&R Construction Services
Civil engineer: G.C. Wallace, Inc.
Landscape architect: SWA Group
Code: Rolf Jensen & Associates, Inc.
Cloud canopy: RWDI

Geotechnical engineer: Terracon Consultants Western, Inc.
Geotechnical/environmental: Zipper Zeman Associates, Inc.
Specifications: Chew Specifications
ADA: Stantec Consulting
Acoustics: Paoletti Associates, Inc.
Entertainment systems: Enterscapes Entertainment
Lighting: Kaplan Partner Architectural Lighting; Lightswitch
Parking: Central Parking System; Walker Parking
Traffic engineer: Gorove/Slade Associates, Inc.
Graphics/signage: Sussman/Prejza & Company, Inc.
Audio visual (structural): Vantage Technology Consulting Group
Audio visual consulting: CM Resources, Inc.
Zoning: Mendenhall Moreno and Associates, Inc.
General contractor: The Whiting-Turner Contracting Company
Photography: Erhard Pfeiffer; Ronald A. Altoon, FAIA

Felipe de Neve Branch Library
Structural engineer: Martin & Huang International
Mechanical engineer: Double O Engineering
Electrical engineer: Nikolakopulos & Associates
Landscape architect: Melendrez & Associates
Civil engineer: Mollenhauer, Higashi & Moore, Inc.
Specification: Ralph P. Mellman & Associates
Artist: Joseph Pinkelman
Photography: Erhard Pfeiffer; Ronald A. Altoon, FAIA

The Gardens on El Paseo
Structural engineer: Brandow and Johnston Associates
Mechanical/plumbing engineer: Store, Matakovich & Wolfberg
Electrical engineer: Nikolakopulos & Associates
Civil engineer: ASL Consulting Engineers
Code/fire protection consultant engineers: Rolf Jensen and Associates, Inc.
Landscape architect: Design Workshop
Specifications: Ralph Mellman and Associates
Specialty lighting designer: Patrick Quigley and Associates
Traffic/parking: Linscott, Law & Greenspan
Parking consultant: Walker Parking Consultants
Geology and soils engineers: Earth Systems Consultants
Public art artist (water sculpture): Mineko Grimmer
Art coordinator: Mary E. Dolden-Veale
Artist: Mineko Grimmer
General contractor: Snyder Langston Real Estate & Services
Photography: Erhard Pfeiffer; Ronald A. Altoon, FAIA

Grand Avenue Urban Design Plan/PACLA
Workshop design team: Frank O. Gehry & Associates, Inc.; Arata Isozaki & Associates; Jose Rafael Moneo; Olin Partnership; Stuart Ketchum
Structural engineer: Nabih Youssef & Associates
Landscape architect: Olin Partnership
Urban design consultant: 34th Street Partners
Traffic engineer: The Mobility Group
Graphics: Bruce Mau Design & Landor Associates
Parking consultant: International Parking Design, Inc.
Construction manager/estimating: PCM
Environmental consultant: Sapphos Environmental
Architectural illustration: Scott Lockard, Lockard Creative

Ka'ahumanu Center
Structural engineer: Robert Englekirk, Inc.
Mechanical engineer/subcontractor: Critchfield Mechanical, Inc.
Electrical engineer: Moss Engineering
Civil engineer: Ronald M. Fukumoto Engineering, Inc.
Soils engineer: Dames & Moore
Traffic engineer: Austin, Tsutsumi & Associates, Inc.
Cinema architect consultant: Eugene E. Leucht Architects, Ltd.
Code consultant engineer: Rolf Jensen & Associates, Inc.
Landscape architect: Tongg Clarke & McCelvey Landscape Architects
Lighting designer: Wheel Gersztoff Friedman Shankar, Inc.
Specifications: Ralph P. Mellman & Associates
Fabric roof: Birdair, Inc.
Construction manager: KX Corporation
General contractor: Keller Construction/U.S. Pacific Builders, Inc.
Photography: David Franzen, Kailua, Hawaii; exterior at night photo courtesy Birdair

Knox City Centre
Associate architect: Hames Sharley International Ltd.
Structural/civil engineer: Bonacci Winward
Mechanical/electrical engineer: Simpson Kotzman Pty. Ltd.
Landscape architect: Tract
Fire engineer: ARUP Fire
Specialty lighting: NDY Light
Quantity surveyor: Rawlinsons Pty. Ltd.
Traffic: Grogan Richards Pty. Ltd.
Hydraulics: C.J. Arms & Associates
Vertical circulation: Transportation Design consultants Pty. Ltd.
General contractor: ProBuild
Photography: Stuart Curnow, Melbourne, Australia; Ronald A. Altoon, FAIA; William J. Sebring, AIA

Kowloon Station Development
Associate architect: Leigh & Orange Architects Ltd, Hong Kong
Associate architect: AGC Design Ltd., Hong Kong
Master plan architect: Terry Farrell & Partners, Hong Kong
Master plan authorized person: Kwan Architects
Structural engineer: Ove Arup & Partners, Hong Kong
Mechanical/electrical: Parsons Brinckerhoff (Asia) Ltd., Hong Kong
Acoustic engineering: ARUP Acoustics, Hong Kong
Quantity surveyors: Levett & Bailey Chartered Quantity Surveyors Ltd., Hong Kong
Traffic engineer: SPB, Hong Kong
Landscape architects: EDAW EarthAsia Ltd., Hong Kong & Irvine, CA
Lighting designer: Francis Krahe & Associates
Graphics: Selbert Perkins Design, Santa Monica, CA
Architectural illustration: Scott Lockard

Macy*s Prototype
Structural engineer: Nabih Youssef & Associates
MEP engineer: Thermaltech Engineering
Civil engineer: Paller-Roberts Engineering, Inc.
Landscape architect: LRM
Cost estimating and specifications: Lonestar Services
Interior: FRCH Design
Code review: Rolf Jensen & Associates
General contractor: Swinerton & Walberg
Photography: Erhard Pfeiffer

MCA Universal Offices
Structural engineer: David D.B. Johnson
Mechanical engineer: Store Matakovich & Wolfberg
Electrical engineer: Nikolakopulos & Associates
Acoustical consultant: Marshall Long Acoustics
Code consultant: Rolf Jensen & Associates, Inc.
Fixtures, furniture and equipment: Freeman Designs
Cost estimator: William F. Mullen
Contractor: Ray Wilson Company
Photography: Erhard Pfeiffer

Nieuw Hoog Catharijne
Architect of record: van den Oever – Zaaijer en Partners Architecten
Project management: Diepenhorst de Vos en Partners
Structural consultant: Van Rossum Amsterdam BV
Mechanical consultant: Techniplan Adviseurs BV
Environmental consultant: Peutz BV
Computer visualization: DPI Animation House

PacifiCenter
Civil engineer: Kimley-Horn Associates
Landscape architect: SWA Group
Geotechnical engineer: Leighton & Associates
Traffic engineer: Crain & Associates
Architectural illustration: Ian Espinoza Associates, Glendale, California

Paramaz Avedisian Building – American University of Armenia
Associate architect/architect of record: LV + Architects
Project manager: GMX Construction, Inc.
Sponsor: Edward Avedisian
Sponsor: Municipality of Yerevan, Robert Nazarian, Mayor
Building committee: Armen de Kiureghian, Ph.D., Professor, University of California, Berkeley Civil Engineer College; Michael Bade, Assistant Director, Design & Construction Services, University of California Office of

Consultants and Collaborators 255

the President, Planning, Design & Construction; Craig Avedisian, Attorney at Law, Law Offices of Craig Avedisian
Engineering services: Arup
Engineering service in Yerevan: Arm Projekt

Les Portes de Gascogne
Architect of record: Sutter & Taillandier
Landscape architect: Agence Laverne Payagistes
Architectural illustration: Michal Suffczyński, Warsaw, Poland

Sengkang Station
Associate architect: 3HP, Singapore
Lighting consultant: Francis Krahe & Associates, Inc.
Photography: Albert Lim KS, Singapore

Siqueiros Mural Shade Structure
Structural engineer: Structure Technology, Inc.
Code consultant: Rolf Jensen & Associates, Inc.
Color interpretation of original mural by David Alfaro Siqueiros: A Espinoza; Los Angeles, California
Model Maker: Alek Zarifian
Photography: Mark Lohman, Los Angeles, California

Southwestern University School of Law Library
Structural engineer: Englekirk & Sabol Consulting Engineers, Inc.
MEP: Store Matakovich & Wolfberg
Civil engineer: Mollenhauer, Higashi & Moore, Inc.
Fire protection/code consultant: Rolf Jensen & Associates, Inc.
Program management: Peck/Jones
Interiors consultant: Freeman Designs
Lighting designer: WGSS
Specifications: Ralph P. Mellman Associates
Contractor: Pueblo Contracting Services
Photography: Erhard Pfeiffer; Wayne Thom

Taman Anggrek Condominiums
Associate architect: 3HP, Singapore
Structural engineer: Martin, Middlebrook & Louie
Mechanical/electrical engineer: PCR Engineers Pte Ltd
Code/fire protection: Rolf Jensen & Associates, Inc.
Parking consultant: Kaku Associates
Landscape architect: Emmet L. Wemple & Associates
Lighting designer: Theo Kondos Associates, Inc.
Ice skating rink consultant: Paul J. Ruffing, AIA
Fountain/water feature: Aquatic Design Group
Graphic designer: David Carter Design Associates
Photography: Erhard Pfeiffer
Architectural illustration: Robert De Rosa, Los Angeles, California

The Shops at Tanforan
Structural engineer: Robert Englekirk, Inc.
MEP engineer: Store, Matakovich & Wolfberg
Civil engineer: Brio Engineering
Fire/life safety: Rolf Jensen & Associates
Soils engineer: Kleinfelder
Landscape architect: LRM Ltd.
Traffic: DKS Associates
Parking: Cary Kopczynski & Co., Inc. P.S.
Graphics: Redmond Schwartz Mark Design
Lighting designer: Francis Krahe & Associates
Specifications: Chew Specifications
Construction management company: CM&D
General contractor: The Whiting-Turner Contracting Company
Photography: Wayne Thom; Ronald A. Altoon, FAIA

UCLA Arthur Ashe Student Health & Wellness Center
Structural engineer: Brandow & Johnston
MEP: Store Matakovich & Wolfberg
Civil engineer: RBA Partners, Inc.
Specification writer: CMS Consultants
Photography: Erhard Pfeiffer

UCLA John Wooden Recreation Center North and West Expansions
Structural engineer: Brandow & Johnston
MEP engineer: Store, Matakovich & Wolfberg
Fire/life safety: Rolf Jensen & Associates
Specification: CMS Consultants
Soils report: Geobase, Inc.
Photography: Erhard Pfeiffer; Wayne Thom

UCLA Parking Structure 3
Structural engineer: Englekirk & Sabol
Mechanical/electrical/plumbing: Store Matakovich & Wolfberg
Civil engineer: RBA Partners, Inc.
Landscape architect: LRM, Ltd.
Contractor: Ray Wilson Co.
Photography: Erhard Pfeiffer

UCSB California NanoSystems Institute
Design architect: Venturi, Scott Brown and Associates, Inc.
Laboratory design: AHSC McClellan Copenhagen
Audio visual/theater design: Auerbach • Pollock • Friedlander
Structural engineer: John A. Martin & Associates
Mechanical/electrical: M-E Engineers, Inc.
Civil engineer: Penfield & Smith Engineers & Surveyors
Geotechnical engineer: Fugro West, Inc.
Landscape design: Wallace Roberts & Todd, Inc.
Parking consultant: International Parking Design, Inc.
Traffic engineer: Orosz Engineering Group
Acoustical engineer: McKay Conant Brook
Vibration/noise control: Colin Gordon & Associates
Lighting: Horton Lees Brogden Lighting Design, Inc.
Signage: Kaminski Kaneko Design
Fire/life safety: Rolf Jensen & Associates
Curtain wall consultant: DVV Associates
Specifications: ANC Specifications Consultants
Cost estimating: Davis Langdon Adamson
Aerial survey: Pacific Western
Photography: Wayne Thom
Architectural illustration: Ian Espinoza Associates

USC School of Social Work
Structural engineer: Englekirk and Sabol
MEP: S&K Engineers
Civil engineer: RBA Partners, Inc.
Landscape architect: Melendrez Design Partners
Fire protection/code: Rolf Jensen & Associates, Inc.
Geotechnical engineer: Geotechnologies, Inc.
Lighting design: LightVision, LLC
Specifications: Chew Specifications
Construction cost estimator: C.P. O'Halloran Associates
Contractor: Hamilton Construction
Photography: Wayne Thom

Victoria Gardens
Executive architect: KA Inc. Architecture
Design architects: Field Paoli Architects & Elkus/Manfredi Architects Ltd.
Structural engineer: Thorson Baker and Associates, Inc.
Mechanical/plumbing engineer: S.Y. Lee Associates
Electrical engineer: Patrick Byrne & Associates
Civil engineer: MDS Consulting
Geotechnical engineer: RMA Group
Landscape architect: SWA Group
Lighting designer: Kaplan Gehring McCarroll Architectural Lighting
Environmental graphics: Redmond Schwartz Mark Design
Traffic engineer: The Mobility Group
Construction manager: Vratsinas Construction Company (VCC)
Construction: Forest City Commercial Construction Co., Inc.
Photography: Erhard Pfeiffer; Wayne Thom; Aerial by night courtesy Forest City Development

Warringah Mall
Associate architect (Phase I): Thrum architects Pty Limited
Associate architect (Phase II): Woods Bagot Pty. Ltd.
Structural engineer: Hyder Consulting Australia Pty. Ltd.
Electrical engineer/lighting designer: Barry Webb & Associates (NSW) Pty. Ltd.
Code consultant: Scientific Services Laboratory
Interior design: MBBD
Landscape architect: Site Image
Quantity surveyor: Rider Hunt
Traffic: PPK Environmental & Infrastructure Pty. Ltd.
Fabric roof: Birdair, Inc.
SpaceTech: Victoria, Australia
Operations: Resolve Engineering
General contractor: Bovis Construction
Photography: Stuart Curnow; Ronald A. Altoon, FAIA

Yassenevo
Associate local architect: Mos Project – 2

Ronald A. Altoon, FAIA James F. Porter, AIA Harvey R. Niskala, AIA Gary K. Dempster, AIA Carl F. Meyer, AIA William J. Sebring, AIA Randy C. Larsen, AIA James C. Auld, Jr., AIA Evelyn Abramson Leticia Aclan Vivien Adao Dale Addy Emily Altoon Eric Altoon Ryan Altoon Bryoe Ambrazienas William Anaya Stephen Andrews Ileana Apostol Paula Arviso Troy Auzenne Vaughn Babcock Darlene Bailey Theresa Baker Jason Balinbin Darrell Bandur Gaila Barnett Thomas Bastis Jeffrey Bautista JoDee Becker Ronald L. Benson, AIA Humberto E. Bermudez Tina Bernardo Laura Berner Erlinda C. Berrios Giovanni Bignasca Chrissie Blaze Annemiek Bleumink Dee Ann Bollow Andre P. Briscoe Guy Matthew Buckles, AIA Arthur D. Buczek Rafael Caballero Ellen Cabrerra Ruben Catabas Sandra Cervantes-Caraballo Ian Cha Fandi Yuen Yi Chan Margaret T. Cheung Donna Chinchar Sakkanon Chirathivat Sam Chou Jin Chun E. Cialic Dan Cockrell Rosie Contreras Lisa Marie Cor Alison Covert Romulo Cruz Timothy C. Cruz Binh T. Dang Ann Davidson Delores Deck Michael Delaney Adriana Donea Suzanne Dvells Marjan Ebrahimi Moon Song Empig Paul H. Enseki, AIA Layla Eyermann Leslie Fernald Diego Fernandez Maria Figueroa Nidia Figueroa Jeff Fineman Julie Flattery Hillary Fleischer Maria Flores Jack Fong, AIA Susan Ford Cindy Fox Aida Gabaldon Art Garcia Victor A. Garcia Marvin Ginsberg Robert Glennie Naura Heiman Godar Ian Gold Erwin Gomez Hector Gomez John Gormley, AIA Barrington Gowdy David Green, AIA Delphine Gregoire David Greunke Kenneth Grobecker, AIA Eva Grycz David W. Hall Megan Hamlin Philli Han James Hansen, AIA Antoine Har Tracey Hardwick Tiffany Hartley Lo Ann Hashimoto Andre Helfenstein Ja Hendricks Glen Anthony Hensle Jessica S. Hensley Hans Herst Cind Hoebink Shannon Holderman Willia Huang Joost Hulshof Ronald Hutchens, AIA Matthew Imadom Maryati Imanto Stephen Ip Chacko Jacob Charles Johnson Mohan Jos Kevin Joyce, AIA Arlene S. Juan Pete Jung C. Karung Louis A. Kaufman, A Greg Keating Robin Kerper Frederic P. Kerz, AIA Kazuhiro Kibuishi D Hyoung Kim Joshua L. Kimmel Jeann Kinney Satsuki Kitagawa Ann Knudsen, AIA Mary Kopitzke Gary Krenz, AIA Pamela Ku Richard L. Ku Hendra Kusuma Daniel Kwok Jul Lamprecht Kim Landau Roi Lapeyr Alison Larsen Masi Latianara Mitchel Lawrence, AIA Charles Lee Manki Le Stella Lee Stephanie Leedom Raymon Leung Jill Lewis Paul Li Chin K. Lim, A Eric H. Lin I-Joen Lin Fang Liu Le Livshetz Kenneth R. Long, AIA Nan Long Denise Loza Chen Lu Frank Lu Rm Madale Christine Magar Daryl Maguire, ANZIA Klayden Malekpoura Rudy Marin Steven McEntee Carm McFayden Kenneth McKently Sabrin Medrano Gaylord Melton Angel Mercer Carinne Meyer Colette Meye Douglas B. Meyer, AIA Frederick Meye Neelam Mian Ellen Miller Blyth Million Hiroko Miyake Arnie Mo Catherine D. Morado Yunjoo Namkoon Matthew Nelson Alleta Nesbit Lourde Nishi Michelle Niskala Cindy Ng Un Ngu Charles W. "Duke" Oakley, FA